Healing From Grief:

Transform Your Pain Into Purpose and Honor Your Loved One

By Kayla Brissi

Copyright

Healing from Grief: Transform Your Pain into Purpose and Honor Your Loved One

Copyright © 2020 by Highly Favored Publishing LLC

ISBN: 9780578667225
Printed in the United States of America
First Printing: 2020
Publisher: Highly Favored Publishing LLC

Cover Design: Mariam Abid
Editing: Rebecca Camarena of Rebecca's Author Services

Dedication

In memory of my Dad, Dale Paulin. Without you, your unwavering belief in me, and constant loving nudge, this book wouldn't be in existence. May our story and journey comfort others and support them to turn their pain into their purpose.

Acknowledgments

Writing a book is not for the faint at heart, but it's also one of the most rewarding life experiences! This book would not have been possible without the support of the incredible people in my life who believed in me even when I didn't always believe in myself.

To my husband and son, I love you both beyond measure. I am grateful you were part of this journey through all of the ups and downs. I know it wasn't always easy between the late nights on the computer and tight deadlines to meet with the book; or the emotional rollercoaster that comes with healing from grief, but thank you for your love, patience, and support while I healed and birthed this dream.

To my mom and sisters, thank you for listening to my *crazy* ideas, reading my writing, lending an ear or a helping hand, and your willingness to explore with me the holistic and alternative methods of healing that have found their way inside of this book.

To Ardyce, my dear friend, with whom I am so grateful that God put you into my life, thank you for always lifting me up in prayer, our insightful conversations, and your loving support in everything I do. You hold a special place in my heart, and I appreciate you so much.

To Ilean (Rhianna) Hill, I genuinely believe the stars aligned for me to meet you. Without the life-changing experience I had with you, I would not have embarked on this spiritual journey or embraced my awakening. Thank you for opening my eyes to what I cannot *see* and delivering my dad's heartfelt message from above that opened my heart to believe.

To Rebecca Camarena, my friend, editor, and book coach - who is always willing to do her part, whether it be to read or edit my writing, coach me or lend a friendly ear, thank you. It is with your steadfast support that my writing career has blossomed into what it is today.

To Sonika Krüger, you are a ray of sunshine, and I am blessed to have you in my life as a client, colleague, and, more importantly, a dear friend. You have been part of my journey and have seen me fall, pick up the pieces, and continue to inspire others no matter how messy things got in my life. Thank you for your willingness to lift me up in prayer, lend me an ear, or offer your profound wisdom. Your support has been invaluable, and it's an honor to have you contribute the foreword for this book.

To my past and current mentors and clients, and fellow colleagues, your contributions to my life have been invaluable. I am blessed to have you in my life, supporting, encouraging, and believing in me. Thank you.

Contents

Foreword

My name is Sonika, and as a fellow coach, I have watched and journeyed alongside Kayla.

Having been a coaching client of Kayla's and having experienced her support, this is my way of thanking her for her constant and loving nudge during our time together.

There are numerous people out there who could have written this foreword, but this honour was bestowed on me. With a Degree in Theology, I have seen how to heal holistically from grief, as well as ways on how to bury grief and not deal with it.

As a personal development coach, I know the importance of making the most powerful choices in life that are supportive and conducive to healing, growth, and transformation. It all starts with the question - are you ready to let go of what doesn't serve you anymore? When you let go of what doesn't serve your highest good, you can be open to receive what is meant for you.

As a fellow spiritual warrior, I am writing this because I believe this book and work is very much needed. Especially when we find ourselves in a new normal way of life. Life as we know it has changed in leaps and bounds these last couple of years. As life changed, so did the people, and with it, the way we experience faith and spirituality.

Kayla shares from her own experience and in her beautiful way with words shows us that healing is a journey. It is not something that happens overnight.

As a unique human being, so will your healing - be unique. For this journey to be powerful and transformative, it is important to honour yourself and take care of your needs during this process, so that you can honour your loved one.

Kayla is a typical Type A personality, driven, and a perfectionist. In her own mind, she declared that she needs to be strong, she is the rock that forms the foundation of support and the glue that keeps her family together. Instead of crying, Kayla made all the necessary phone calls and arrangements. Instead of being with her heartache, she was doing. Instead of being vulnerable, she was striving.

Maybe you are this way as well? Or you know of someone who is always on the go and not settling to experience their emotions and grief. Then this book is perfect for you or as a gift for a loved one. It is written in short, easily digestible chapters.

In Healing from Grief, Kayla shares the seven stages of grief, but with two powerful add ons that will allow you to experience a powerful healing journey, to help repair your broken heart, find your inner spiritual warrior, and support you in turning your pain into power.

I come from the wonderful world of ministry, but my career was taken away from me 18 months ago. I didn't take the time to fully process my emotions, because it was after all a choice that I made. It was the best choice at that moment, but it wasn't what I had desired for my life.

I didn't take the time to grieve and cry for a career that I loved. This grief manifested in uncomfortable ways. Just as Kayla will share her own story of mental health, I also had to seek help for anxiety and depression.

It was a painful process for me.

To seek help, I first had to accept my situation and sit with my emotions. And only after accepting those emotions could I seek the help and support I needed.

Kayla shares profound ways on how to support yourself. I want to encourage you to be open and curious about the things she is sharing. It might make you feel uncomfortable, but sit with that feeling and then explore the possibilities.

When I made the powerful choice to live from a place of love rather than fear, I began to feel at peace within myself. I felt at home. The feeling of peace allowed me to explore the possibilities.

As Kayla guides us in Healing From Grief, one of these possibilities is to transform our pain into purpose.

What is your purpose?
What are you called for in this life?

When we experience loss, we don't want to think that it can be for the Higher Good. We can get stuck in a place where we think - why is God doing this? What did I do to deserve this?

You did nothing to deserve it. God is not punishing you in any way.

No matter who or what you lost in your life, you are allowed to grieve. You can be heartbroken, and you can cry yourself to sleep every night. Your emotions are as valid as everyone else's. This is a process. Your grief story and the journey are just as unique as you are.

Dealing with loss is painful and challenging. This book is written to help you navigate the uncertainty. It gives words and actions to emotions that might be too big to understand or even describe.

There is no right or wrong way of dealing with your emotions. Just as there is nor right or wrong way to journey with your grief.

Maybe you are new to grief, or maybe your grief has surrounded you like a stuffy coat on a hot summer's day. It doesn't matter where you are in your grieving journey, I want to honour you for taking the first step in healing. What you are holding in your hands will gently and lovingly nudge you forward. One step at a time.

Once you start to transform your pain into purpose, you will enjoy a spiritual awakening. Lean into God. Tune into yourself and determine what you believe is true for your journey.

Healing from grief will give you the strength to be your own person again.

Accept where you are on your journey. Be open and curious about new ways to heal from your grief. Trust yourself on this journey, but trust that there is purpose in your pain. Know that you are not alone, you are surrounded by loved ones, seen and unseen. Your journey is about honouring yourself and the one you lost.

There lies power in your choices, make the one that is the most empowering choice. Love. Love is always the better choice.

When I experienced the loss of my career, Kayla was a loving and caring guide. She helped me to see the purpose in my pain. Kayla was not just my coach, she is my friend as well. I saw her journey from heartbreak and pain to triumphant and purposeful.

As a Reformed Reverend, I was skeptical and uncertain about the woo-woo, but I remained open and curious. I test everything I hear and read. I just don't accept it as the truth. This is the one thing that Kayla and I have in common, be curious but not irresponsible.

When Moses and the Israelites were having a war in the desert, Aaron saw that when Moses kept his arms in the air, the Israelites won, but when he got tired and let his arms down, the Israelites lost. Aaron held up Moses' arms until the battle was won. As a spiritual warrior, I have the responsibility to keep your arms high when you are in battle. Know that I will keep you in my prayers as you are on this journey from grief to healing.

You are not alone.

Kayla, you are more than just an author and a coach. You are my friend! And I am so damn proud of you!

Sonika Krüger
Personal Development Coach
sonikakruger.com

Introduction

"Grief never ends, but it changes. It's a passage, not a place to stay. Grief is not a sign of weakness, nor a lack of faith. It is the price of love."

- Author Unknown

When I look back on my life and the last year I spent with my dad, there are things I would have done differently; moments I should have cherished more than I did, things I wish I would have said and didn't, and treatment options I could have explored but didn't.

Should've, would've, could've...hindsight is always 20/20. While I could dwell on all of the things I wish I could go back in time to fix, I simply cannot. And that's the thing about grief, some days you feel as if you are on a hamster wheel going a mile a minute just trying to make it through the day and the next the thought of getting up is unbearable. You know life must go on, but the invisible pain is sometimes too much to bear.

When my dad passed in May 2017, my heart shattered into a million pieces. Each day since his passing, I envision my heart being repaired with gold lacquer like the Japanese tradition Kintsugi (kin-tsu-gee). I pick up one broken piece and seal it with the others, knowing that one day my heart will be whole again. It won't be pristine, but it'll visibly show the pain of my past and its healing journey. It'll serve as a constant reminder of what I lost, and the same goes for you too.

Know that I am in the trenches with you, and this book will serve as your survival guide while you battle the war on grief. You can read it front to back or choose to read the chapters that will most meet your needs at any given moment. Within the pages, you'll find inspirational quotes, practical healing methods, exercises for you to explore, and recommended resources.

My hope is that it'll help repair your broken heart, find your inner spiritual warrior, and support you in turning your pain into your purpose so that you can live a highly favored life while still honoring your loved one.

With love and gratitude,

Kayla

Disclaimer

The information provided in the book is for general informational purposes only. All information is provided in good faith, however, we make no representation or warranty of any kind, express, or implied regarding the accuracy, adequacy, validity, reliability, availability, or completeness of any information provided.

The information provided is not intended to diagnose or prescribe any treatment for any medical or psychological condition(s), nor does it claim to prevent, diagnose, treat, mitigate, or cure any medical or psychological conditions.

It contains ideas and opinions of the author and is intended solely to provide helpful information on a variety of subjects. It is sole with the understanding that the author and publisher are not engaged in rendering medical, health, or any other kind of personal professional services in the book.

The reader should consult his or her medical, health, or other competent professional before adopting any of the suggestions in the book with regard to their health.

The author and publisher specifically disclaim all responsibility for any liability, loss, or risk, personal or otherwise, that is incurred as a consequence, directly or indirectly, of the use and application of any of the contents of this book.

Bonus Materials

Firstly, THANK YOU for purchasing Healing from Grief. It is my sincere desire to be as helpful to you as possible during this time, and I'm looking forward to sharing some practical and useful insights with you throughout the book.

As a bonus, I have several resources that I have pulled together for you. Please navigate to my website at intuitivespiritualwarrior.com, where you will find various downloadable documents for you to print and use, a meditation or two, as well as links to products I recommend for your healing journey, and more.

To grab your bonuses, all you need to do is join our online community at https://bit.ly/HealingFromGriefBonuses, and you'll receive instant access and the password to view them.

Also, at the back of the book, I have provided information for various grief and bereavement support professionals to assist you on your journey. It's not an exhaustive list, but they are ones I feel would be the most beneficial for you, and they are in one spot to find for easy reference.

Thanks again for allowing me to be on this journey with you!

Part 1 - Grief

"Grief is the last act of love we have to give those we loved. Where there is deep grief, there was great love."

\- Author Unknown

Chapter 1

What is Grief

Grief, what is it? It is a natural response to loss and is an extremely personal experience for people regardless of where their pain stems from. It's a rite of passage, so to speak, that we all go through in this journey of life.

Its reactions can be felt like a direct response to physical causes, like the death of a loved one or beloved pet, or through symbolic or social losses, such as divorce, loss of finances, health, independence, or a job.

Each kind of grief represents something that was taken away from a person. While people experience various types of loss throughout their life, the experience itself is vastly different and can trigger particular grief reactions. These reactions can be emotional, mental, physical, social, or even spiritual.

For example, psychological reactions, referring to emotional and mental issues, can include anxiety, sadness, despair, guilt, or anger. Physical responses may include changes in appetite, causing weight gain or loss, illness, or problems with sleeping. Social reactions typically include troubles returning to work or being around loved ones. Lastly, spiritual reactions may consist of blaming God, distancing yourself from your faith, or even leaving the church altogether.

These reactions can cause significant problems in the griever's life, especially if they don't seek support. Ultimately, it's a domino effect. If the griever does not address the underlying issue, the cause for the grief, then more problems will continue to compound until they burst like a shaken up pop bottle.

Furthermore, it's important to note that while your grief experience may be similar to another's, it is entirely unique to you. How you grieve, what you experience, the length of time you take to heal, is entirely up to you.

No two people have the same journey, not even family members who have lost the same loved one. Trust me, as I know from personal experience, and if a professional tells you otherwise, quite frankly, they're wrong.

If you were to do a quick Internet search for the stages of grief, you would find a variety of articles, illustrations, and diagrams. Some even make it seem like everyone's grief journey is the same - linear. Unfortunately, that simply is not true. It's more like a tangled mess where you zig-zag in every which direction in no particular order. And the not so fun part about the zig-zagging is it can happen at any time when you least expect it. Awesome, not.

Chapter 2

What are the Stages of Grief

A s mentioned previously, your grief journey and the stages in which you zig-zag through are anything but linear. However, what are the stages of grief, and how do you know which stage you're in?

For starters, let's break down each stage and then delve deeper into identifying them.

In 1969, Elisabeth Kübler Ross first identified the five stages in her book, *On Death and Dying*. The five stages are denial, anger, bargaining, depression, and acceptance. Furthermore, other grief experts argue that there are seven stages of grieving, which are shock, denial, bargaining, guilt, anger, depression, acceptance.[1]

However, I feel there are truly nine stages of grief. I can attest to the validity of the seven stages of grief because I experienced them first hand, but I do feel that once you reach acceptance, there's also transformation and purpose.

Moreover, it's important to note that not everyone will experience all nine stages of grief during their healing journey. You may revisit some multiple times and keep in mind that to experience the stages they are not in a perfectly linear fashion, you will ping back and forth like a ball in a pinball machine.

Now, let's explore each of the stages based on my interpretation of each.

Shock

Shortly after the loss of a loved one, the bereaved often experience shock. Shock is most commonly associated with the news of one's sudden death, but not in all cases. In my experience, the shock is a natural response to loss and usually accompanied by a period of disbelief that the death is true - a feeling as though it's a nightmare that you'll simply wake up from soon.

When you are experiencing shock, your symptoms will vary. Still, the most common is the inability to eat or drink, insomnia, temporary immobility or paralysis while trying to process the shock, screaming out loud, shaking of the body, rapid pulse and breathing, cold, clammy skin, and more.

These symptoms often feel intense on an emotional and physical level that can be draining to the bereaved. Although they're exhausting, the good news is this stage typically doesn't last for an extended period - more like several days versus months.

However, keep in mind that you can circle back to feelings of shock at any point in your healing journey. While it's most common to be the first stage you experience after the death of a loved one, it won't be a once and done sort of thing. You inevitably will zig and then zag back into this stage multiple times. This is normal as your healing journey is not linear, and how you grieve is unique to you.

Denial

Denial is often associated with the next stage you experience after the shock stage. While I can agree to a certain extent, I know it's not the case for everyone.

When in the denial stage, it's a period of coping and survival. The goal is to simply get through the day while still mourning the loss of a loved one. The days are often a blur, and living can even feel pointless or daunting. However, even when there is doubt, there is grace.

This stage doesn't particularly have symptoms, so to speak, but more like actions to be aware of. Such as avoiding the topic of the loved one's death, refusing to touch or move their personal items, acting as if the deceased person is still physically here, not facing the facts, unwillingness to accept reality, and more.

It's important to note that denial is a healthy response to allow your mind the mental space to unconsciously absorb the information at a pace that won't send you into a downward psychological spiral. When and if this should happen, the denial stage can become unhealthy, and the bereaved should seek professional support.

Bargaining

The bargaining stage is a period where the bereaved try to understand the situation within their mind and review how they could have done things differently or better, so their loved one would still be alive. It's a stage full of helplessness, vulnerability, and emotional turmoil.

When in this stage, the bereaved often try to negotiate with loved ones or their higher power, such as God, with a little quid pro quo or spiraling downward with the "what ifs."

All of which is an attempt to repair the broken heart. The goal is to regain control of their life that feels as though it's crumbling into pieces so they can rebuild its structure and feel whole again.

Guilt

The guilt stage is an interesting one, it's full of shoulda, woulda, coulda.

This stage, too, is about control. Rather than trying to rebuild the structure or foundation like denial, this phase is more focused on the need for control and order.

When in this stage, the bereaved can feel immense guilt, whether it be rational or irrational, but their mind tries to justify or process the loved one's death. The irrational thoughts arise to find just about anything to feel guilty about, such as getting a second opinion or trying a different treatment and believing it could have worked to save their life.

This dissecting every moment with a loved one is time-consuming! While it's a necessary process for our healing, it's essential to know that staying in this stage for an extended period does not serve your highest good.

Anger

Anger is an inevitable feeling when it comes to grief. The bereaved often feel anger towards themselves, their deceased loved one, other family members, medical professionals, God, and more or any combination of them at once.

Anger has no boundaries; therefore, it can wrap its claws around whoever is within its reach with a firm grip!

While all the stages are essential for healing, this one I feel is where you reach the point of a possible breakthrough. Allowing yourself to truly feel the anger and work through the pain you feel from the loss is vital to the healing process. The deeper the pain from the grief, the stronger the anger.

Depression

The depression stage is a dreadful state to be in when it comes to your healing journey. While I wish I could tell you this phase is all rainbows and unicorns, it, naturally, is not.

While in this stage, the most common signs are significant feelings of despair, frequent negative thoughts, intense sadness, uncontrollable emotions with both highs and lows, withdrawing from loved ones, increased tiredness, possible insomnia, and more.

Unfortunately, when you reach this stage, do not be alarmed if you stay in this stage for a more extended period. However, with that said, this stage is vital to the growth you will experience for healing; it's important to also acknowledge when you need to seek professional help for severe depression or potential suicidal thoughts.

Acceptance

Acceptance in and of itself is a milestone. This stage is often associated with the notion that everything is going to be alright and embracing the "new normal" - life without your loved one.

It's important to note that you may never feel ok with the absence of your loved one, and that's perfectly normal. You can accept and understand that despite the loss, you will be alright, and life must go on.

When in this stage, the bereaved must embrace the new normal and learn to live their life without them in it. Remembering a world with their loved one in it is ok, but if they strive to continue to live as if they're still living, it is not healthy. It's time to recalibrate - live a vibrant life!

Transformation

The transformation stage is most likely to occur towards the end of the healing journey once you have accepted the loss of your loved one. However, know that you will be on a transformative journey throughout the entire healing process. This continual transformation will come in ebbs and flows that much like a wave will carry you onto the shore where it's calm.

Once you're fully in the transformation stage, it is here where you find clarity, a sense of peace, and inner knowing that will lead you to find your purpose in how you will honor your loved one and their legacy.

Purpose

Much like the transformation stage, the purpose stage will be ever-evolving, and you won't realize it at the time, but your grief healing journey will eventually lead you to find your purpose. When you look back on your journey, and through finding clarity, you'll soon connect the dots. It will simply click and make sense.

When you fully immerse yourself into the purpose stage, you will have newfound meaning to your loved one's death. You'll desire to honor them and their legacy. There's a renewed sense of hope and passion that comes from experiencing deep inner pain and a longing to keep their memory alive. When you acknowledge the feeling and accept the call, you spring into action and begin the process.

Chapter 3

Are You Coping with Grief

D ealing with the loss of a loved one is inevitably the most painful and challenging experience you will have throughout your lifetime. Grieving is a natural human experience; there's no right or wrong way to grieve, so to speak. It can't be rushed, and there's no specific timeline for mourning your loss. Over time, healing gradually occurs.

How you grieve also depends on various factors, such as your personality, life experience, faith, depth of your loss, or method of coping.

Are you coping with your grief?

At first thought, you would probably immediately say yes, but how do you know if you genuinely are coping?

When you are coping with your loss, you will experience some or all of the following:

- Awareness of your mental health status to identify grief versus severe depression.
- Seeking support and are not afraid to ask for help during this significant life transition.

- Accepting the facts and knowing your loved one is gone.
- Understanding your grief journey is unique to you.
- Acknowledging the pain from your loss and feeling the emotions as they come.
- Taking care of yourself - mind, body, soul, and spirit.
- Releasing yourself of any guilt and pain because of the circumstances.

It's important to know that grief also presents physical symptoms, such as fatigue, rollercoaster emotions, changes in weight and eating habits, nausea, compromised immunity, and insomnia, to name a few.

How do you know if you're not coping appropriately with your loss? In short, you're doing the exact opposite of what I mentioned above. Your life is in disarray. Extreme sadness, withdrawing, avoiding people, places, and things, for example.

When you are not healthily coping with your grief, it's vital to acknowledge that you need professional help to support you in healthily dealing with your pain.

Chapter 4

Myths About Grief

U nfortunately, society and our loved ones place unrealistic expectations on the bereaved in how they should grieve. The reality is they often make our grief journey more challenging, and rather than helping us, they're causing more pain and anguish. With these unrealistic expectations, we tend to set unrealistic expectations for ourselves, which only further complicates our healing journey.

I like to call these unrealistic expectations as myths. They're considered a myth because they're not universally true. Does that mean they apply to everyone or that they're never accurate? No, but for the majority of grievers, they're merely false.

Therefore, let's debunk some of these grief myths because I do not want you to fall into the trap of these unrealistic expectations and feel as though you need to accept them as truth. Know that this is not an exhaustive list of myths, but they are the most common ones that you will likely have while healing from your grief.

Grief only lasts for a short time.

You and I both know this definitely isn't the case. Grief has no timeline or endpoint. It's something you experience, and it'll stay with you until it's your time to be called home to be with our Lord.

The first year is the hardest.

Admittedly, yes, the first year is definitely challenging, but let's not dismiss the others. You will have moments where you succumb to your emotions and experience grief as if it was yesterday despite how long it has been that they passed.

Time heals all wounds.

I do believe time does repair wounds, but not necessarily heals all wounds. Your heart was broken into a million pieces. As you piece it back together, it'll never look or be the way it was before the loss. It'll simply be mended, but still fragile.

Displaying photos of your deceased loved one or talking about them, or keeping personal belongings, means you're not processing your grief.

Good grief, displaying your photos, talking about them, or keeping some of their personal belongings does not mean you're stuck or not healthily processing your grief. It shows that you want to honor your loved one, and there's absolutely nothing wrong with keeping their memory alive. That's all part of mourning their loss and a standard process to grief.

Once you go through the stages of grief, you're healed.

While I wish I could say this is 100% true, it isn't. As previously mentioned, you will have days where you will succumb to your emotions and mourn your loved one's death as if it were yesterday. You will go through the stages multiple times and zig-zag from one to the other. In the early part of your healing journey, you'll experience the stages of grief quickly and more intensely. Over time, you'll likely notice a gap between them or that they won't last for long periods.

If you're still grieving after a few months, you're playing the victim.

Grief has no timeline or boundaries. The length of time it takes you to grieve is unique to you. No two people grieve the same, and therefore, the expectation that you should be back to normal after a few months is a joke. Most likely, you're not playing the victim; it's called mourning.

You need to just get over it because they're not coming back.

Admittedly, this one makes my blood boil. No, you can't just move on or get over it with a snap of your fingers. Grief is real, the pain is internal, and the sadness is eternal. You will not wake up one day and no longer miss your loved one. There will always be a part of you that misses them, but you cannot avoid living your life. As part of your healing journey, you will learn to live without them but still honor their memory.

There's a prescription for grief.

Yes, there are prescriptions available, if needed, to support you with medical conditions that can arise as a result of grief such as anxiety, depression, PTSD, or trauma. However, no pill can cure your grief. You are in control of your healing journey, and it requires an internal transformation that does not come in a pill container.

All grief is the same.

No, absolutely not. You can grieve for a variety of reasons, not just death, and each one of those situations you will experience a different form of grief. Also, to reiterate, no two people grieve the same, therefore, while someone may be sympathetic to your loss and feel that they understand what you are going through, they simply do not. Their journey was unique to them, just like yours is unique to you - not the same.

If you don't cry or bottle up your emotions, you'll grieve quicker.

Oh boy, this is the exact opposite of the truth! For starters, not everyone cries when they're grieving, and that's perfectly ok. When it becomes an issue is if they're pushing those emotions aside and not allowing themselves to feel them and embrace the healing journey. I can attest to the fact that bottling up your feelings, keeping busy, or avoiding the pain will likely end in a disaster - a breakdown. This breakdown could be emotional or mental, or it could cause significant issues with your relationships, career, faith, etc.

Chapter 5

Christian Beliefs about Death, Grief, & Loss

Our lives are full of happiness and sorrow. There are moments when we feel full of joy and other times when we feel the pain of regret - grief has unbearable pain at times and is full of sadness.

During moments like these, as Christians, we often turn towards God and lean on Him for guidance, peace, and comfort. It's important to consider how we, as Christians, often grieve as we delve into the topic of death, loss, and grief.

The Bible reminds us that God is in control, and when we experience the loss of a loved one, it is a blessing to grieve according to our beliefs. How do Christians grieve? While I cannot speak on how every religion chooses to honor the dead, I can discuss with you what the Bible offers for valuable advice for Christians to follow. Let's take a brief look at a couple of scripture verses.

Brothers and sisters, we do not want you to be uninformed about those who sleep in death, so that you do not grieve like the rest of mankind, who have no hope. For we believe that Jesus died and rose again, and so we believe that God will bring with Jesus those who have fallen asleep in him. According to the Lord's word, we tell you that we who are still alive, who are left until the coming of the Lord, will certainly not precede those who have fallen asleep. For the Lord himself will come down from heaven, with a loud command, with the voice of the archangel and with the trumpet call of God, and the dead in Christ will rise first. After that, we who are still alive and are left will be caught up together with them in the clouds to meet the Lord in the air. And so we will be with the Lord forever. Therefore encourage one another with these words. 1 Thessalonians 4:13-18

Blessed are they who mourn, for they will be comforted. Matthew 5:4

What are these bible passages telling us about death and grief? Quite simply that it's acceptable to grieve, and we are encouraged to mourn our loss because we will be comforted. We may not grieve in the same manner as others, but we have hope that our loved one will rise and wait for us in the Kingdom of Heaven.

We are also reminded of the death and resurrection of Jesus Christ. He died, rose from the dead, and his redemption is a promise to us believers that we, too, will have salvation - everlasting life.

Although our loved ones are no longer with us, they have not ceased to exist. They will forever be in our hearts and with us in spirit. We will meet them again, but for now, mourn their loss, embrace the sadness and sorrow, and hold firmly on to your faith as it will bring hope during these challenging times.

Part 2

My Backstory

"There is a sacredness in tears. They are not the mark of weakness, but of power.
They speak more eloquently than ten thousand tongues.
They are messengers of overwhelming grief...and unspeakable love."

- Washington Irving

Chapter 6

My Spiritual Journey

━━━━━━━━ ❧❦❧ ━━━━━━━━

I have been Catholic my entire life. While I wish I could say that I am a *Saint,* I am not. I have challenged God, lost my faith over the years, and ultimately grew closer to Him. What changed? I did!

Before my dad's passing, I would consider myself to be a practicing Catholic. I went to church nearly every Sunday, prayed daily, started studying the Bible, and did my best to follow the Christian way of life. Could I have been a better Christian? Admittedly, yes, but isn't that the point? Strive to do better than the day before - be more Christ-like.

After my dad's passing, I regretfully admit my relationship with God became strained. Going to church became a trigger for me where I would succumb to my emotions, and my dad's funeral would play like a movie in my head.

However, my life changed when God aligned the stars for my mom and me to attend a Mind, Body, Spirit Fair. My mom was interested in seeing a medium to connect with my dad. I, on the other hand, was skeptical and scared out of my mind. Not wanting my mother to go alone, I mustered up the courage to take her while arming myself with my rosary and wearing a cross necklace for protection.

As I sat across the room from the medium, I studied her, trying to gauge her authenticity. With my stomach churning and feeling in knots, I watched and listened to her deliver messages of love, hope, and inspiration to strangers who too lost a loved one. Despite witnessing her giving heartfelt messages from above, I couldn't help but still feel skeptical and wondered if my dad would have a message for me.

Moments later, our eyes met from across the room and I got caught off guard by what she said next.

"As I come to you, wow, you have some real powerful spirit guides on the other side. They come marching in like soldiers. What is this about? It's pretty amazing!"

Hallelujah, I exclaim!

"Do you get in touch, thinking about them or connecting with them?"

No, I'm too busy, I reply with a nervous chuckle, and I sheepishly look down at the floor.

"Yeah, that's the message here. You are too busy. They really want your attention. The fact that they come in like soldiers, there's gotta be a reason for this - that maybe they're bringing you strength for something. Is that something you need right now?"

I reply, probably, with my chin quivering and tears welling up in my eyes.

"Strength to be your own person again. You know we all need to focus on our own authenticity. Especially as women as we're always doing more for others. We're worn out some days and that's not ok."

"I see a cheek close to you. A male loved one from the other side. I see him standing between the two of you, and his cheek is so close to yours." As she points in my direction to my left cheek.

"Did you lose a male loved one?"

Yes, my father recently passed, I anxiously share with her.

"You need to know that he's doing better than you are. He's saying, "What's the matter with you? Don't you believe in heaven? Don't you believe in good things, God, the spirit world?"

I sat there in awe; the way she delivered that particular message sounded exactly like my late father. I eagerly waited for more.

"Are you expecting something - more responsibility? What I hear them talking about is that you need to start delegating with a firm hand. Whatever that means, but I'll leave that with you."

I couldn't believe it, and I burst into tears.

My life was about to change, and my journey to healing from my grief started soon after that. Meeting this medium, I believe, was a divine intervention, where she was placed in my life at the exact moment I needed her.

The beautiful moment we shared as she delivered messages from above was beyond what I ever thought possible, and it opened my heart and the proverbial doors to my healing journey. I cannot deny what I have personally experienced and witnessed. They say, seeing is believing, and I 100% believe that!

A year later, my mom and I attended another event. I realized that as I walked around the room amongst the other healers and spiritualists that I felt at peace - home. I no longer felt like an outcast or guilty like I was doing something wrong, like the last event, or that it was all "too out there" for me. Interestingly enough, my perspective changed, and the idea of embracing more of the "woo-woo" Spiritualism didn't seem so odd to me anymore. I eagerly walked around to each booth, observing the vendors, and taking it all in, so to speak. I watched various healers work their *magic*. I listened and learned and absorbed as much information as I could because I was intrigued.

After witnessing another accurate mediumship reading for my mom from my dad, I decided to receive a reading too. She sat in front of me, and a short time later began pointing at me exactly as my dad would when giving me one of his many lectures. He would tower over me with his right-hand pointer finger and thumb aiming directly at me. Like one of his Ruger handguns, making his infamous hand gesture of disapproval moving up and down rhythmically, like a woodpecker pecking wood, with his booming voice piercing my ears as he states his dissatisfaction with my decision. I sat in awe, and what she said sent chills down my spine.

"What are you doing? I taught you better than that! Stop letting people walk all over you!"

I guarantee the look on my face was priceless!

As crazy as it sounds, my dad found a way to lecture me from beyond the grave. I knew that if two complete strangers could deliver messages from above with 100% accuracy that this wasn't a joke!

A couple of months later, I happened to meet another medium, and she opened the spiritual door more fully, and it was then that I began to experience unexplainable things myself. At the start of our relationship, I committed myself to be open to learning more and "going all in," so to speak, without judgment.

Within the first couple of weeks of working together, she challenged me to write in my journal to my dad to see if he would communicate. Not knowing what I was doing or if I could even receive a message, I decided to give it a try because I committed to being open-minded, and at this point, what did I have to lose?

After saying a prayer, asking for protection, and getting into a meditative state, I simply ask - Dad, are you here? Can you give me a sign? At this point, I felt foolish and was struggling to wrap my head around the concept that our loved ones are still amongst us after they die. I felt a mix of emotions, hopeful but also very skeptical that this would work, but I patiently waited for a sign so that I could journal my question to him.

Moments later, I distinctly felt a shove at the lower part of my back. Thinking I must be losing my mind and it's a coincidence, and asked if it was my dad to do it again. A few seconds later, I felt a forceful shove to my wrist with such force; it kicked it out from beneath my head, causing it to drop onto the couch. Gathering my thoughts and repositioning my head, I lay there still in disbelief.

I asked for the third time for him to prove to me if he was here with me. Boy, oh boy, did he ever give me a sign! Within seconds I felt hard shoves on my upper back, right wrist twice, my lower back, and legs as if he was poking at me playfully.

Startled, I sat straight up with chills running down my body. It took me a moment to register what happened. How is this even possible? Am I going crazy? Trying to rationalize what I just experienced, looking to see if it all was my imagination or a mere coincidence. It wasn't.

Each shove felt precisely as they did growing up when my dad would give us a playful push when goofing around with us. There was no mistaking that it was him. I knew beyond a shadow of a doubt we were communicating, and I could not deny that he was there with me.

Days later, she challenged me to read cards and insisted that I could read them intuitively. Not believing her, I rolled my eyes at the mere thought of me having any such spiritual gifts. However, unbeknownst to me, I did possess such a gift and delivered accurate readings providing details on things that I could not possibly know anything about to complete strangers.

They were just as astonished as I was.

Over the next few days, she taught me to communicate with my dad through the use of a pendulum as a form of dousing. Seeing the pendulum move entirely on its own with accuracy was mind-boggling! Every question I threw at it returned an accurate answer.

My eyes were wide open, and I could no longer deny that I, too, was blessed with spiritual gifts and that there are spirits among us but, more specifically, our deceased loved ones.

Like a flip of a switch, my grief seemed to shut off. I was at peace, knowing my dad was still around me in spirit and that I could communicate with him any time I wanted or needed. A huge weight was lifted off my shoulders, and I was finally feeling hopeful about the future. I wasn't alone.

Because of this entire spiritual journey and unbelievable experiences, I found that my faith and beliefs expanded and strengthened. I have never felt more close to God than before, and I finally understood that this, too, is all part of my grief journey - part of our story.

If you're anything like me, a Christian, you probably think that this goes against your religious beliefs, it's demonic, ungodly, a sin, etc. Trust me, I genuinely understand as I was one you. From the start of my journey, I promised myself that I would not do anything that didn't align with my beliefs. Therefore, it forced me to do my research so that I could fully understand what I was getting involved in as I embarked on this journey.

I admit I wrestled with my beliefs and upbringing of the church. I scoured the Internet for research about spiritual gifts, communicating with spirits, and what the Catholic church says about it all. After reading several articles, I honestly felt horrible about myself as a Christian. Learning that many Christians see these gifts as demonic, ungodly, new age, not biblical, etc. was rather heartbreaking and confusing. Why would God give anyone these beautiful gifts if it wasn't for the good of His people?

I decided that I had to make a choice about my beliefs. I began to review all of them to determine if it was something I truly believed in my heart or if it was a belief that was bestowed upon me through outside influences such as my parents, loved ones, the church, and more.

What I came to understand and accept is that our beliefs are often shaped by influences both consciously and subconsciously, but at the end of the day, we must lean into God, tune into ourselves, and determine what we believe to be true in our heart.

For me, beliefs go far more profound than being able to quote the Bible or following the teachings of your church. While those are important, there's so much more to it than that. It's a feeling deep within your soul that guides you as an inner GPS.

Once I accepted that I could have both religious and spiritual beliefs, I no longer felt at war with myself. I wasn't feeling judgmental about other religions, non-believers, spiritualists, and viewed everyone as equal because we're all connected. I have witnessed miraculous things in my life and know the power of receiving God's grace. There's no denying that he is very much a part of my life.

Moreover, if you take a look at various religions, you will notice that each has their own set of beliefs. Does that mean that any particular one of those religions is better than another or right versus wrong? No, it merely means they believe something different than another, but the one common denominator is God. He is the link that binds us together in love.

Furthermore, if you are feeling uneasy about the conversation of spiritual gifts and the like, I want to encourage you to dive deeper into the Bible as this is the word of God. You will find some scripture verses that talk specifically about spiritual gifts and communicating with spirit. Now how you interpret them may vary slightly from myself or another, but the point is that these topics are not "new age," like many Christians believe. How could they be if they're in the Bible, the one facet of Christianity that is common amongst religions? It's because it isn't.

I understand that this all may seem too farfetched, trust me, I was that way also. All I ask is that you receive this information with an open heart and mind. You may be surprised to find that you, too, are a gifted servant of God and that perhaps in your heart of hearts, you believe something different than what the church has taught you.

Did you know the Bible supports the fact that there are people who possess miraculous spiritual gifts and can be contacted by spirits? It sure does! Those that have these extraordinary gifts have a responsibility to use them as God intended them to do to serve Him and his people.

Perhaps as a Christian, you have experienced extraordinary occurrences that you cannot explain. Maybe you even have spiritual gifts that you are either aware or unaware of, like me. Do you feel insecure or uncomfortable about sharing your experiences with others in fear they wouldn't believe you, that you will be condemned or chastised by the church? Most likely, yes, because I felt that way too.

However, I want to encourage you to share these experiences and gifts with others. You may find that one of two things happen:

1. You will empower others to share their experiences and further strengthen their relationship with God.
2. You will find that you are not alone that others, too, possess spiritual gifts from God and willingly embrace them.

Furthermore, there are familiar scripture verses that are the most frequently cited when the topic of spiritual gifts arises amongst Christians as it's often a taboo topic for many based on what they have been told to believe about them.[1] They are as follows:

- Do not turn to mediums or seek out spiritists, for you will be defiled by them. I am the Lord your God. Leviticus 19:31
- I will set my face against anyone who turns to mediums and spiritists to prostitute themselves by following them, and I will cut them off from their people. Leviticus 20:6
- 'A man or woman who is a medium or spiritist among you must be put to death. You are to stone them; their blood will be on their own heads.' Leviticus 20:27
- Let no one be found among you who sacrifices their son or daughter in the fire, who practices divination or sorcery, interprets omens, engages in witchcraft, or casts spells, or who is a medium or spiritist or who consults the dead. Anyone who does these things is detestable to the Lord; because of these same detestable practices the Lord your God will drive out those nations before you. Deuteronomy 18:10-12
- When someone tells you to consult mediums and spiritists, who whisper and mutter, should not a people inquire of their God? Why consult the dead on behalf of the living? Consult God's instruction and the testimony of warning. If anyone does not speak according to this word, they have no light of dawn. Isaiah 8:19-20

I admit, reading and hearing them made me fearful too. The verses make it out to be that communicating with spirits or using your gifts is a sin or that *all* spirits are ungodly. Some Christians may even believe if they show any interest or use their gifts that they will somehow displease God and find themselves in hell or turned away from their church.

Firstly, I do not believe that to be true. If you are a Christian, you speak and follow the word of God, and have a pure loving intention, then I do feel that you are His servant and are meant to share your unique gifts with others.

Secondly, the unfortunate thing about those scripture verses is that if you were to read what the actual passages are referencing and their context, you would notice that they are not aligned. Therefore, they're an invalid biblical reference of the Bible to support one's beliefs that any unusual spiritual gifts are not from God.

Proverbs 3:5-6 states, Trust in the Lord with all your heart and lean not on your own understanding; in all your ways submit to him, and he will make your paths straight. Meaning, put your trust in Him to guide you, not anyone else. That's the type of relationship he wants with you. He doesn't want you to seek other people and worship them as another God.[1]

Additionally, in Joel 3:1-2, it says, And afterward, I will pour out my Spirit on all people. Your sons and daughters will prophesy, your old men will dream dreams, your young men will see visions. Even on my servants, both men and women, I will pour out my Spirit in those days. What this scripture says is that God will not discriminate in who will receive the gift of the Holy Spirit or spiritual gifts.[1]

Let's delve deeper into scripture because you will interestingly find how the Bible further supports what we're discussing and debunks the beliefs of many who claim to know the biblical truth about spiritual gifts.

To start, in 1 John 4:1-3, it states, Dear friends, do not believe every spirit, but test the spirits to see whether they are from God, because many false prophets have gone out into the world.

In 1 Peter 3:18-19, it said, For Christ also suffered once for sins, the righteous for the unrighteous, to bring you to God. He was put to death in the body but made alive in the Spirit. After being made alive, he went and made proclamations to the imprisoned spirits.

Lastly, John 4:24 says, God is spirit, and his worshipers must worship in the Spirit and in truth.

Therefore, riddle me this - If we are to avoid spirits as mentioned in the previously noted Leviticus scripture, then why are we to "test the spirits" in

1 John? If Jesus himself preached the good news about the Kingdom of Heaven to spirits, as stated in 1 Peter, then why are we to not communicate with them also as a follower of Christ? Furthermore, how are we to worship God as a Christian if we are to avoid any contact with spirits. Isn't God himself the trinity - Father, Son, and Holy Spirit? If you avoid any contact with a spirit, then you ultimately are avoiding contact with God.[1]

1 Thessalonians 5:19-22 says, Do not quench the Spirit. Do not treat prophecies with contempt but test them all; hold on to what is good, reject every kind of evil. Meaning, test everything, accept the Holy Spirit, honor God, and reject anything that is ungodly or evil.[1]

Therefore, it is apparent that Christians should not avoid *all* spirits or avoid those who possess the spiritual gift that allows them to communicate with spirits. If we reject communication with spirits, we then reject the Holy Spirit, and thereby inadvertently reject God, his teaching, guidance, and ability to serve as he intended for us to honor Him.[1]

Moreover, what does the Bible say specifically about spiritual gifts? You may be surprised to find that within its pages, it discusses thirty-one spiritual gifts. You'll find them all listed below within the following scriptures.

Dream Interpretation

Pharaoh said to Joseph, "I had a dream, and no one can interpret it. But I have heard it said of you that when you hear a dream you can interpret it." "I cannot do it," Joseph replied to Pharaoh, "but God will give Pharaoh the answer he desires." Genesis 41:15-16

Craftsmanship

Then Moses said to the Israelites, "See, the Lord has chosen Bezalel son of Uri, the son of Hur, of the tribe of Judah, and he has filled him with the Spirit of God, with wisdom, with understanding, with knowledge and with all kinds of skills— to make artistic designs for work in gold, silver and bronze, to cut and set stones, to work in wood and to engage in all kinds of artistic crafts. And he has given both him and Oholiab son of Ahisamak, of the tribe of Dan, the ability to teach others. He has filled them with skill to do all kinds of work as engravers, designers, embroiderers in blue, purple and scarlet yarn and fine linen, and weavers—all of them skilled workers and designers. Exodus 35: 30-35

See the Unseen

When the servant of the man of God got up and went out early the next morning, an army with horses and chariots had surrounded the city. "Oh no, my lord! What shall we do?" the servant asked. "Don't be afraid," the prophet answered. "Those who are with us are more than those who are with them." And Elisha prayed, "Open his eyes, Lord, so that he may see." Then the Lord opened the servant's eyes, and he looked and saw the hills full of horses and chariots of fire all around Elisha. 2 Kings 6:15-17

Enjoying Work

Moreover, when God gives someone wealth and possessions, and the ability to enjoy them, to accept their lot and be happy in their toil—this is a gift of God. Ecclesiastes 5:19

Justice

In that day the Lord Almighty will be a glorious crown, a beautiful wreath for the remnant of his people. He will be a spirit of justice to the one who sits in judgment, a source of strength to those who turn back the battle at the gate. Isaiah 28:5-6

Revealing Mysteries

The king asked Daniel (also called Belteshazzar), "Are you able to tell me what I saw in my dream and interpret it?" Daniel replied, "No wise man, enchanter, magician or diviner can explain to the king the mystery he has asked about, but there is a God in heaven who reveals mysteries. He has shown King Nebuchadnezzar what will happen in days to come. Your dream and the visions that passed through your mind as you were lying in bed are these. Daniel 2:26-28

Courage

But as for me, I am filled with power, with the Spirit of the Lord, and with justice and might, to declare to Jacob his transgression, to Israel his sin. Micah 3:8

Exhortation

Strengthening the disciples and encouraging them to remain true to the faith. "We must go through many hardships to enter the kingdom of God," they said. Acts 14:22

Prophecy, Serving, Teaching, Encouragement, Giving, Leadership, and Mercy

We have different gifts, according to the grace given to each of us. If your gift is prophesying, then prophesy in accordance with your faith; if it is serving, then serve; if it is teaching, then teach; if it is to encourage, then give encouragement; if it is giving, then give generously; if it is to lead, do it diligently; if it is to show mercy, do it cheerfully. Romans 12:6-8

Word of Wisdom and Knowledge (Psychic), Faith, Healing, Miraculous Powers, Discernment, Speaking and Interpretation of Tongues

Now to each one the manifestation of the Spirit is given for the common good. To one there is given through the Spirit a message of wisdom, to another a message of knowledge by means of the same Spirit, to another faith by the same Spirit, to another gifts of healing by that one Spirit, to another miraculous powers, to another prophecy, to another distinguishing between spirits, to another speaking in different kinds of tongues, and to still another the interpretation of tongues. All these are the work of one and the same Spirit, and he distributes them to each one, just as he determines. 1 Corinthians 12:7-11

Apostleship, Helping, and Administration

Now you are the body of Christ, and each one of you is a part of it. And God has placed in the church first of all apostles, second prophets, third teachers, then miracles, then gifts of healing, of helping, of guidance, and of different kinds of tongues. Are all apostles? Are all prophets? Are all teachers? Do all work miracles? Do all have gifts of healing? Do all speak in tongues? Do all interpret? Now eagerly desire the greater gifts. 1 Corinthians 12:27-31

Evangelism, Pastoring, and Ministry

So Christ himself gave the apostles, the prophets, the evangelists, the pastors and teachers, to equip his people for works of service, so that the body of Christ may be built up until we all reach unity in the faith and in the knowledge of the Son of God and become mature, attaining to the whole measure of the fullness of Christ. Ephesians 4:11-13

Intercession

Therefore he is able to save completely those who come to God through him, because he always lives to intercede for them. Hebrews 7:25

Hospitality

Offer hospitality to one another without grumbling. Each of you should use whatever gift you have received to serve others, as faithful stewards of God's grace in its various forms. 1 Peter 4:9-10

As you can see, the Bible supports various spiritual gifts. The beautiful thing about this is every single one of us possesses one or more of the amazing gifts!

Therefore, to reiterate my point, how can we deny those who have unique spiritual gifts such as the ability to communicate with spirits or the gift of prophecy when the Bible talks about these gifts in great detail and in support of them?

Is it plausible your church has chosen to ignore the word of God and not embrace the spiritual gifts bestowed upon its members but rather teach they are sinful? Yes, it's entirely possible which is why it is important for you to dig into the word of God and determine what you believe to be true in your heart.

With that said, I want to leave you with one final scripture verse before we move onto the next chapter.

Don't be deceived, my dear brothers and sisters. Every good and perfect gift is from above, coming down from the Father of the heavenly lights, who does not change like shifting shadows. He chose to give us birth through the word of truth, that we might be a kind of first fruits of all he created. James 1:16-18

Chapter 7

My Healing Journey

It was a brisk spring morning in May 2017, when I was in my parent's living room struggling to keep my eyes open due to days without sleep, with a fan blowing on my face, my dad's heart-wrenching moaning piercing my ears, and the loud hum of his oxygen machine drowning out my thoughts. I was anxiously standing next to him in his hospice bed, holding his hand and praying for peace and comfort. At the same time, I looked into his lifeless hazel eyes as he stared off into the distance while he took his last breath, and at that moment, I kissed his forehead and told him, "We love you, Dad."

I took a few minutes to process his death and push back the sudden panic that began to wash over me like tidal waves. I close my eyes, slow my breathing, and count to ten. I give my mom a sorrowful look, grab my phone, and make my way to my parent's bedroom to start making the dreaded calls. Trying to keep it together, my voice cracking from the emotional pain and heartbreak, I dial the numbers to his siblings, coroner, and hospice nurse. As I sit on the edge of my parent's bed, I can't help but feel the weight of the world on my shoulders.

The tragedy of losing my dad most certainly changed the trajectory of my life. Admittedly, I was unprepared for his death, and this has single-handedly been the most challenging thing I have ever had to endure throughout my life.

It almost seems like yesterday that our story began. In April 2016, he received a blessing in disguise that bought us another year with him. As odd as it may sound, I am so grateful for the day that he fell off a ladder at one of my rental properties. Without this accident, his cancer would have gone undetected, and we would not have had one more year to listen to his stories, hear him laugh, or create memories with him.

After the accident, he received a biopsy of his lung at the VA hospital. The results confirmed he had limited-stage small cell lung cancer, a form of aggressive cancer that spreads quickly. Once he received the diagnosis, he was scheduled for surgery to remove the lower lobe of his right lung where the tumor was located. A few weeks later, he started his rounds of chemo and then brain radiation as a preventative in hopes that the lung cancer wouldn't come back with a vengeance.

For most of 2016 and 2017, my life revolved around my dad and his care. I focused on taking him to and from appointments, surgeries, and treatments. Traveling to and from these appointments up to four hours a day and sometimes multiple times a week to ensure that he received the care he needed. Several nights were spent at the VA hospital when he was admitted for a variety of reasons during his treatment.

In January 2017, my dad was experiencing pain that his oncology team couldn't determine the source or cause as his scans were clear, showing no sign of cancer returning. He insisted it was kidney stones, but I believe he knew it was his cancer spreading.

Over the next couple of months, his health worsened. Finally, at my urging request, he agreed for me to take him to the local Emergency Room for a checkup. Intuitively, I knew that something wasn't right, and feared that his cancer returned. The on-call doctor, unfortunately, confirmed my worst fear while I sat in a patient room #12 with my parents. Together we learned his cancer spread to his liver, kidneys, and into both lungs. As I looked at the images with the doctor, I could not believe how much cancer his body had

- it was everywhere! I stood there looking at the computer in shock, wanting to believe my eyes weren't seeing the massive amounts of tumors lingering in his body.

I looked over at my parents while I took dubious notes from the doctor, and the expression on their faces is one I will never forget. It was as if their brains weren't processing the information. I repeated to them what the doctor said a few times, but perhaps the shock of the news was too much for them to fully understand the diagnosis, I'm not entirely sure.

The next morning, I contacted his oncology doctor and rushed him to the VA hospital for more tests and observation. We spent the night, and the following morning his oncology team confirmed that in fact, his cancer has spread and that his time with us would be cut short. How short, we weren't entirely sure.

At the hospital, I sat next to my dad's bed with my Mom on the other side of it, and I tried with all my might to hold back the tears. I did not want my dad to see how upset I was about knowing he was dying. The thought of losing him was unbearable, and I wanted to scream out in agony.

I glance in my dad's direction to see him sitting with his hands together on his lap and a stoic expression on his face. He never cried or showed that he was afraid to die. Truthfully, I never saw such bravery as I did while I watched his life deteriorate before my eyes. He accepted his fate and was ok with it by reminding me that he lived a good life, and it was his time to go.

While we waited for him to be discharged, we had many challenging discussions about what to do next. Once released, I was able to bring him home and admit him to hospice. The ride home was unbearable, and I was a blubbering mess in the back seat. The pain of knowing his death was imminent was almost paralyzing, and I kept replaying a conversation we had in my head.

I was in the chair next to his hospital bed, taking notes while he gave me instructions for what to do after he was gone, and he turned to face me and with an oddly calm expression on his face. He said, "Well, kiddo, I only have three more days left to live." Interestingly, he passed three days later, surrounded by his loved ones.

In my mind, I always was convinced that my dad would grow old with my mom, death is what happens to others, but not me. My dad was my rock, my hero, my go-to person for everything. No matter what mess I got myself into, or repairs needed or lectures to dole out - he was there.

I didn't know grief could be this painful - emotionally, mentally, physically, and spiritually. It's as if you are at war with yourself, and it's a losing battle! With my broken heart, there's an emptiness that longs for my dad. No matter how hard I try to fill the void, I cannot; it's a bottomless pit - a vast, deep dark hole that will forever remain empty.

In the beginning, I looked for signs that he was still around and never saw any, but now, I know what I overlooked or often dismissed as coincidences. For a while, I attempted to replace the emptiness of pain with something else, but it never worked. I tried to go about my life, embracing the new normal, a life without him in it, and pray that I would feel whole again one day.

When I started on my healing journey, it was rough, to say the least. I didn't process my emotions and kept them bottled up inside. I isolated myself, shut out my family and friends, and could barely keep it all together. I was too proud to admit that I, the "strong one," the glue that holds the family together, and the rock that forms the foundation of support, needed help.

My life became like a train wreck, where I experienced severe exhaustion, lacked concentration, inability to focus, experienced forgetfulness, and lost all creativity. I struggled with the inability to cope with extreme and debilitating anxiety, where it felt as if an elephant was sitting on my chest suffocating me. Extreme mood swings, negative thoughts, self-sabotage, and lack of interest in everything became a regular occurrence in my life. I was barely eating, felt weak, and struggled to care for myself.

Ultimately it led to my emotional and mental breakdown. After I snapped at my son, I quickly realized I needed help. I found myself in the doctor's office being prescribed massive doses of medication for major recurrent depression and generalized anxiety disorder while discovering I also had signs of post-traumatic stress disorder (PTSD).

I graciously accepted the help while fully knowing that over the coming months, it would be my mission to eliminate the need for any prescribed medication. After my spiritual awakening, I embarked on a holistic healing journey that allowed me to wean off of the medicine and utilize alternative and holistic methods to support my healing.

I aspire to use my experiences and story to help others who are going through a similar situation to me to learn how to holistically heal (with the support of a proper professional). What we are about to embark on together is my process for healing from grief. Let's dive in!

Part 3

A Practical Guide to Healing From Grief

"I know you feel broken, so I won't tell you to have a wonderful day.
Instead I whisper these words to you 'just hold on'.
As the darkest days of grief start to get less, the sun will rise again for
you."

- Zoe Clark-Coates

Chapter 8

Meditation & Mindfulness

As part of your healing journey, incorporating meditation and mindfulness is a crucial component and, in my opinion, the foundation for your healing. This is truly a powerful way to find some serenity amidst the storm.

There are several benefits to meditation; in fact, there are irrefutable science-based facts! According to Healthline Media[1], the science-backed benefits include:

- Reduces stress
- Controls anxiety
- Promotions emotional health
- Supports self-awareness
- Increases mental clarity, focus, and attention span
- Reduces memory loss
- Aids in fighting addiction
- Promotes love and kindness
- Improves sleep
- Supports pain management
- Decrease blood pressure
- Supports overall health and well-being

Not only that, but meditation can be done anywhere and by anyone to improve emotional and mental health. It's free and doesn't require you to be a pro either. Pretty much a win-win, in my opinion!

Mindfulness is a state of being consciously aware of something from a nonjudgmental lens, and it's intentional. Therefore, when it comes to emotional management, it is essential to be mindful of your surroundings and the situation that is causing you to experience negative emotions.

It is often associated with intention, awareness, observation, and acceptance. Let's explore each a little bit further.

Intention

Intention is focusing on the present moment without thinking about past or future events.

Awareness

Tuning into your five senses intentionally and mindfully to what is happening in the present moment.

Observation

Recognizing the world around you with your five senses and tuning into the positive and negative thoughts, sensations, or feelings that arise, observing them without reaction or judgment, and acknowledging them for what they are.

Acceptance

Accepting what you can or cannot control, and that includes what you may be experiencing through your five senses, without trying to change it, your reactions, or with judgment.

Since we are talking about meditation and mindfulness, we also need to discuss mindful meditation. What exactly is it? Mindful meditation typically involves breathing exercises, mental imagery or visualization, awareness of your body, mind, and five senses to promote body relaxation. The goal is to slow down racing thoughts, release negative emotions or feelings, calm your mind and body.

It doesn't require any fancy equipment, but if you want to use candles, essential oils, crystals, etc., you're welcome to add them to the meditation process. As for preparation, you simply need a comfortable place to sit, five minutes of free time, and a judgment-free mindset.[2]

Next, let's explore how to meditate. Below you will find a step-by-step guide to mindful meditation.

1. Find a comfortable place to sit that feels calm and relaxing for you.
2. Determine how long you plan to meditate. If you're a beginner, choose a shorter time frame, such as 3-5 minutes. A timer is recommended so that you can focus and not worry about the time.
3. Close your eyes and ground yourself using the 5-4-3-2-1 grounding technique that is widely used by psychologists and behavioral specialists (with a slight twist).
    o Five things you SEE.
    o Four things you FEEL.
    o Three things you HEAR.
    o Two things you SMELL.
    o One thing you find POSITIVE about yourself, situation, or your surroundings.
4. Set an intention and say a prayer.
5. Notice your body and its state.
6. Slow your breathing and inhale for 3 counts and exhale for 3 counts.
7. Follow the sensation of the breath as you inhale and exhale.
8. Notice when your mind wanders and redirect your focus to breathing.

9. Close with kindness and gratitude by making note of your surroundings, how you feel, what you're grateful for, etc.

These are the basics to meditation, mindfulness, and mindful meditation. Mindfulness is something you can do throughout your day. Make note of when you are present in the moment and when your attention is elsewhere. It'll help you zero in on where to redirect your time and attention to people, places, things, etc. that are important to you.

It's recommended that you set aside time daily to practice mindful meditation. Start with 3-5 minutes and grow from there. The more you engage in this practice, the longer you will be able to meditate.

Chapter 9

Journal Writing

When you are experiencing and healing from grief, you undoubtedly will have moments when your mind cannot stop thinking about your loved one, where you will want to scream out in frustration, and also times when you feel entirely alone. It's painful, I understand entirely, but know that this too shall pass.

An excellent way to help you process your emotions, clear your mind, support your healing journey is to use a journal. The benefits of journal writing are to keep your thoughts organized, record milestones or special events, boost or improve memory, relieve stress, promote self-reflection, manage negative emotions, and support healing.

This journal is yours to do with what you wish. You can keep it to yourself, show others, or whatever else your heart desires. Additionally, you can use a fancy journal you purchase, a regular school notebook, type it into a document like Microsoft Word or Google Docs, or use an online journal program.

To start using your journal, you will want to commit to writing in it daily. If you desire your journal to be more of a "Dear Diary"-like, you're welcome to do that, but for me, I just write whatever comes to mind and not worry so much about structure, grammar, or spelling. Let it flow!

Choose a time of day to journal and block off at list 15-minutes daily to write. The time of day you choose to write in your journal will likely vary based on your schedule or the best time to practice self-care and self-love. Yes, journal writing is a form of self-care. I recommend either morning or evening journal writing. Could you do both? Yes, something I often recommend for my clients, but if you know you can only commit to one time of day, then choose which ones make the most sense to you. If it doesn't work out, you can always change it!

Below are some journal prompts to help you get started.

- I'm really missing…
- The hardest thing about losing my loved one is…
- The most challenging time of day is…
- I find it helpful when…
- I find it challenging when…
- I am grateful for…
- My favorite memory of my loved one is…
- Today I was triggered by…
- My support system includes…
- I wish my loved ones would say…
- When I'm alone, I feel…
- The things that help me the most right now are…
- I feel…
- I remember…
- I hope…
- I love it when…
- The things that bring me joy are…
- My dream for the future is…
- I'm struggling with…
- I'm afraid that…
- If I could change one thing it would be…
- I feel guilty about…
- My loved one was like…
- I hate it when…
- My loved one always made me laugh when…
- I'm thinking about…
- I'm reminded of my loved one when…
- Something that brought me hope is…
- Something that inspired me is…
- Something I don't want to forget about my loved one is…

As you begin to journal daily, review your entries over time to see the progress you have made and reflect on your transformative journey. Know that there will be bumps in the road, and probably some twists and turns too, but know that you will make it to your final destination.

Chapter 10

Aromatherapy

A romatherapy is an excellent way to provide support holistically for your healing. According to Healthline Media, they state that "Aromatherapy is a holistic healing treatment that uses natural plant extracts to promote health and well-being. Sometimes it's called essential oil therapy. Aromatherapy uses aromatic essential oils medicinally to improve the health of the body, mind, and spirit. It enhances both physical and emotional health."[1]

Aromatherapy has been around for years dating back to the Ancient Egyptians and Greeks. They have been used for medicinal and religious purposes worldwide too. The way aromatherapy works is that it activates the smell receptors in your nose that sends messages directly to your brain's limbic system. This system affects your emotions, memory, learning, appetite, and sex drive. Therefore, inhaling aromas, such as through essential oils or burning incense, stimulate different responses throughout your body that provide a positive healing effect.[2]

They provide several benefits for supporting the mind, body, soul, and spirit; some of which are as follows:

- Improving focus and mental clarity
- Providing a grounding and balance

- Alleviating pain
- Improve sleep quality
- Reduce symptoms of headaches and migraines
- Boost immunity
- Aiding digestive support
- Reduce stress, anxiety, and support other mood disorders
- Reduce the side effects of chemotherapy treatment
- Kills bacteria, fungus, and viruses
- Promote relaxation

There are four aromatherapy ways in which I would like to share with you. They are essential oils, burning of incense, saging, and palo santo.

***

Essential Oils

When my dad was first diagnosed with cancer, I was experiencing frequent anxiety and wanted an alternative to popping a pill. I decided to explore essential oils because they were a safe, natural alternative for me, and I was interested in having him try them too.

After doing some research, I decided to jump on the oil bandwagon and give it a try. To say I quickly became obsessed is an understatement. There's a saying in the essential oil community, "I have an oil for that!" I can't help but chuckle because I often catch myself saying it whenever a loved one or myself needs some extra support.

If you are not aware of what essential oils are, they are compounds that are extracted from plants that capture the essence, scent, or flavor. They are obtained through mechanical or distillation processes for use in one of three ways: aromatically, topically, or internally.

However, I must provide a word of caution, do not ingest any essential oils without the guidance from a professional who understands essential oils and the body. You will find conflicting information about essential oil use and their safety on the Internet, and you must understand the risks.

Furthermore, let's briefly review how to safely use essential oils. Many people often believe that because they are natural, they cannot harm you. That's completely inaccurate. While they are an excellent way to support you, as with anything, there are things to consider for safety.

- Dosage
- Application
- Dilution
- Storage
- Children
- Health Conditions

Dosage

As with anything that promotes health and wellness, essential oils should be monitored and used with the proper dosage guidelines for adults and children. Essential oils are quite potent, and only a small amount of the oil is necessary to achieve the result you are looking for. You must be aware of the dosage recommendations to ensure you are safely using the essential oils. The following is the recommended dosage for daily consumption by dōTERRA®.[3]

- Aromatically: No limits
- Topically: For adults, 12-36 drops or for children, 3-12 drops in 24 hours
- Internally: For adults, 12-24 drops or for children, 3-12 drops in 24 hours

Application

As previously mentioned, there are three ways to use essential oils. - aromatically, topically, and internally. Aromatic use is the process of experiencing the aroma of essential oils through the air by inhaling or breathing in oils, often with the use of a diffuser.

Topical use is the process of applying the essential oils to the skin. Places you can topically use essential oils will vary based on the oil, but here are all of the areas on your body to consider.

- Temples or back of neck
- Behind ears
- Over heart
- Abdomen
- Wrists
- Sole of foot
- Bottom of big toe
- Base of big toe
- Base of pinky toe
- Base of middle toe
- Bottom of middle toe
- Outer arch of foot
- Inner arch of foot
- Heels
- Chest
- Shoulders
- Outside of ears

Internal use is the process of taking the essential oils directly in the mouth, by adding them to food or beverages, or via a capsule and then ingesting them.

It is vital that you have a full understanding of how to use essential oils, their appropriate dosages, risks, and more to ensure you are using them safely for yourself and with your loved ones, including pets!

Dilution

When using your essential oils, it's necessary to follow the guidelines for topical application. Most are safe for use without using a carrier oil, like fractionated coconut oil, but many should be diluted because they are too powerful to put directly onto the skin.

As mentioned, the best way to dilute essential oils is with the use of carrier oils. There are a variety of carrier oils available. They are fractionated coconut oil, sweet almond oil, olive oil, argan oil, avocado oil, and grapeseed oil, to name a few. The vital thing to note is the texture and consistency of the oil, and its odor. I recommend using fractionated coconut oil as a preferred carrier oil.

When diluting, you can follow this rule of thumb:

1 tsp of carrier oil + 1 drop of essential oils = 1% dilution

Storage

Storing your essential oils correctly is vital to keep their potency, efficacy, and safety reasons. Make sure the caps are on tight, store in a cool, dry place, and out of the reach of children.

Children

As noted above, it's necessary to keep your essential oils out of the reach of children because they simply don't understand how to safely use them. Children can use essential oils with adult supervision. It's important to mention that children' have more delicate and sensitive skin than adults, so diluting the oils before use is crucial for safe application.

Health Conditions

As you begin to use essential oils, it's necessary to acknowledge and be aware of your personal health conditions. Some medical conditions are not compatible with essential oils. For example, some essential oils are not recommended during pregnancy because they can cause complications.

Yes, it is safe to use essential oils in conjunction with your regular exercise and diet regimen to promote a healthy lifestyle. However, please be your own advocate for your health and consult a medical professional first to address any health concerns.

Now that we have discussed how to safely use essential oils let's explore which oils would be perfect for you to support you and your grief.[4]

Anger

For support with feelings of anger, use any of the following essential oils:

- Bergamot
- Cardamom
- Cedarwood
- Frankincense
- Roman Chamomile
- Spearmint
- Wild Orange
- Ylang Ylang

Anxiety

For support with anxious feelings, use any of the following essential oils:

- Sandalwood
- Vetiver
- Wild Orange
- Wintergreen
- Ylang Ylang

Broken Heart

For support with mending your broken heart, use any of the following essential oils:

- Geranium
- Lime
- Rose
- Spikenard
- Wild Orange
- Ylang Ylang

Emotional Wounds

For support with deep emotional wounds, use any of the following essential oils:

- Eucalyptus
- Frankincense
- Geranium
- Lime
- Myrrh
- Roman chamomile

Denial

For support with feelings of denial or disbelief, use any of the following essential oils:

- Birch
- Black Pepper
- Cinnamon
- Coriander
- Grapefruit
- Juniper Berry
- Marjoram
- Peppermint
- Roman Chamomile
- Sandalwood
- Spearmint
- Thyme

Depression

For support with feelings of sadness or depression, use any of the following essential oils:

- Bergamot
- Douglas Fir
- Frankincense
- Geranium
- Grapefruit
- Juniper Berry
- Lavender
- Lemon
- Lime
- Patchouli
- Peppermint
- Spearmint
- Thyme
- Tangerine
- Wild Orange
- Ylang Ylang

Grief

For support with feelings of grief, use any of the following essential oils:

- Bergamot
- Cedarwood
- Frankincense
- Geranium
- Helichrysum
- Marjoram
- Lavender
- Melissa
- Rose
- Sandalwood

Guilt

For support with feelings of guilt or shame, use any of the following essential oils:

- Bergamot
- Fennel
- Grapefruit
- Lavender
- Oregano
- Vetiver
- Ylang Ylang

Hopelessness

For support with feeling hopeless, use any of the following essential oils:

- Lime
- Patchouli
- Vetiver
- Wild Orange
- Ylang Ylang

Shock

For support with feelings of shock use any of the following essential oils:

- Bergamot
- Frankincense
- Geranium
- Roman Chamomile

Spiritual

For spiritual connection and support, use any of the following essential oils:

- Cinnamon
- Frankincense
- Juniper Berry
- Roman Chamomile
- Sandalwood

From dōTERRA, I personally recommend their signature blends Balance®, Console®, Forgive®, and Serenity®.

A word of caution, please do not buy your essential oils from your local drugstore, general merchandise store or random online retailers. Many oils sold are not high quality, sourced properly, and are not safe for use. I personally recommend dōTERRA or Rocky Mountain Oils™.

When my dad passed, my mom, sisters, and I were all struggling. I decided to create a unique blend in memory of my dad and to promote emotional and mental well-being. After asking for feedback on a name, my sister suggested Angel Kisses, and I thought it was absolutely perfect! You can find the recipe to make yourself an Angel Kisses Essential Oil Blend rollerball so that you, too, can feel at peace during this difficult time.

Angel Kisses Essential Oil Blend

Ingredients:

- 10 drops Console®
- 5 drops Forgive®
- 10 drops Serenity®
- Fractionated Coconut Oil
- 1-10ml glass roller ball bottle

Instructions:

In a 10 ml glass roller ball bottle, add the instructed amount of essential oils for each of the Console®, Forgive®, and Serenity®. Fill the remainder of the bottle with fractionated coconut oil. Leave a little space at the top to avoid spillage. Place the rollerball and its cap on top of the bottle, and shake slightly to mix the ingredients. Apply as needed.

***

Burning Incense

Burning incense is the second way I utilize aromatherapy for healing, and I recommend you consider it too for your healing journey and support with grief. Incense burning has some of the same effects as essential oil usage in addition to the following:

- Deepen attention
- Heighten awareness
- Aide in spirituality
- Promote mindfulness
- Support meditation
- Stimulate creativity

Moreover, when burning incense, you can use the incense sticks with an incense stick holder if that's your preference or consider my preferred method. I use an abalone shell on a stand with charcoal discs and resin incense.

To use a shell or other fire-safe bowl, you will simply place the charcoal disc at the bottom, light it, and place the resin on top. I also like to gently blow on it to generate the smoke and then fan my hand slowly in front of my face to take in the aroma before placing it down in front of me.

I enjoy burning incense during my prayer and meditation time simply because of the scent that I use. I recommend using frankincense, myrrh, 7 archangels, 3 kings, and copal to start. You don't want to mix them all together, but choose one or two and see if it is something that would interest you. See below for information on each, and it's usage.

Frankincense

Frankincense resin use is for grounding and centering, meditation, spiritual growth, healing, calming emotions, mental focus, and purification. It can also help with feelings of despair and stress, support visualization, and increase mental focus.

Myrrh

Myrrh resin is for use with mediation, peace, purification, healing, and spirituality.

7 Archangels

The 7 Archangels resin includes frankincense, myrrh, benzoin, copal, dammar, sandalwood, and other essential oils. Its use is for peace, meditation, healing, and spiritual growth. As well as for blessing a house, clearing energy, and supporting you during prayer.

The seven archangels are Archangel Michael, Archangel Jophiel, Archangel Chamuel, Archangel Gabriel, Archangel Raphael, Archangel Uriel, and Archangel Zadkiel. Each archangel is associated with a particular color and provides unique support for your healing.

- Archangel Michael is associated with the color blue and offers physical and spiritual protection.
- Archangel Jophiel is connected to the color yellow and offers wisdom.

- Archangel Chamuel is associated with the color pink and offers a resolution in love.
- Archangel Gabriel is connected to the color white and offers guidance and order in one's life.
- Archangel Raphael is associated with the color green and offers healing for the mind, body, soul, and spirit.
- Archangel Uriel is connected to the color red and offers guidance and peace.
- Archangel Zadkiel is associated with the color violet and offers forgiveness.

3 Kings

The 3 Kings resin includes frankincense, myrrh, and benzoin. Its use is for peace, balance, harmony, healing, and spiritual growth.

Copal

Copal resin is often for use with mediation, promoting feelings of love, purification, healing, and spirituality. It can also support depression and infertility, increase confidence and creative expression, aid in manifestation, and provide mental clarity.

You can purchase incense sticks, resin, and the like through various online retailers or even at your local businesses such as rock or crystal shops, metaphysical or spiritual stores, or specialty shops.

***

Burning Sage

Saging has become one of my favorite ways of aromatherapy. Dating back to use with the Egyptians, Romans, and Greeks for medicinal uses as well as within Native American healing traditions it is burned as a possible way to heal, protect, increase wisdom, and guard against disease.[5]

Burning sage is more commonly associated with spiritual rituals and is often known as smudging. While useful for religious ceremonies, there are several other benefits for its use. Such of which include the following.

- Grounding and balancing
- Supporting meditation
- Improving mood and promoting calmness
- Increase in mental clarity and focus
- Reducing stress, anxiety, and depression
- Anti-inflammatory, antioxidant, and microbial support properties
- Cleansing of the air of bacteria
- Improving intuition
- Purification
- Repelling insects

The most common sage to burn is white sage. You could also burn sage with rose petals, lavender, and other herbs bound with it too.

Burning sage is simple, but here are a few guidelines to follow.

1. Use a fire protectant bowl, an abalone shell, or a sage burner to burn the sage. You will want something to catch the ashes as they fall. I use my abalone shell and hold the sides to avoid burning myself from the bottom, getting too hot to touch.
2. Open a window or a door before you start burning the sage so that smoke can exit the home, and you are not inhaling the smoke. For those with respiratory problems, a word of caution with burning sage as it could cause complications.
3. Place the sage in the burning container and light it on a 45-degree angle. Let it burn for a few seconds and then gently blow on it to stop the flame and let the embers begin to smoke. If it stops producing smoke, light it again, and follow the same procedure.

4. If you are burning sage for spiritual reasons, I recommend you take a moment to bring yourself to the present moment, set a positive intention for what you are doing, and say a prayer.
5. When ready, you will walk around to each room, if applicable, or leave it in the place in which you are sitting. Allow the smoke time to enter and fill the room, but be mindful of the amount of smoke and careful with inhaling it too.

As with the incense, you can purchase sage through various online retailers, at your local businesses, such as rock or crystal shops, metaphysical or spiritual stores, or specialty shops. If you're lucky, you could find it in the wild to source, dry, and bundle yourself!

***

Burning Palo Santo

Palo Santo burning is another favorite of mine to burn because not only does it remind me of my dad, but I love the unique scent it emits when lit. It comes from trees grown on the coast of South America and is related to frankincense, myrrh, and copal. It's part of the citrus family and has notes of pine, mint, and lemon. Interestingly, a little known fact, in Spanish, palo santo means "Holy Wood".[6]

As with sage, palo santo has several benefits for its use too. Some of them are the following:

- Relieving cold and flu symptoms
- Reducing stress, anxiety, and depression
- Alleviate headache and migraines
- Anti-inflammatory properties
- Promotes calmness and balance
- Cleansing and purification
- Insect repellent
- Healing

- Spiritual growth
- Deeper connection
- Preparation for meditation

When it comes to burning palo santo, it's pretty much the same as burning sage. For ease, I have provided the instructions and guidelines here for you to use.

1. Use a fire protectant bowl, an abalone shell, to burn the Palo Santo. You will want something to catch the ashes as they fall. I use my abalone shell for this too and hold the sides to avoid burning myself from the bottom, getting too hot to touch.
2. You may choose to open a window or a door before you start burning the Palo Santo, but I don't feel it's necessary as the smoke emission is vastly different than burning sage.
3. Place the Palo Santo in the burning container and light it on a 45-degree angle. Let it burn for a few seconds and then gently blow on it to stop the flame and let the embers to begin smoking. If it stops producing smoke, light it again, and follow the same procedure.
4. If you are burning Palo Santo for spiritual reasons, I recommend you take a moment to bring yourself to the present moment, set a positive intention for what you are doing, and say a prayer.
5. When ready, you will walk around to each room and pause for a minute or two to purify the air, if applicable, or you will leave it near the place in which you are sitting.

Like with sage, you can purchase palo santo through various online retailers, at your local businesses such as rock or crystal shops, metaphysical or spiritual stores, or other specialty shops.

Now that you know how to use various types of aromatherapy, it's time for you to try them for yourself. Choose 1-2 to start and explore how they can support your healing journey.

Chapter 11

Crystals

O h, for the love of crystals! These beauties add a powerful punch to your healing journey. I admit I was a bit skeptical, too, until I kept an open mind to try them. I could not believe the difference in how I felt. In fact, crystals and aromatherapy supported my healing when I weaned myself off of my antidepressant and anxiety medication.

Healing with crystals is an alternative medical technique where they are used to cure and protect against disease and support other medical ailments. Holistic healing practitioners believe crystals act as a conduit for healing by allowing positive healing energy to flow into the body, forcing the negative energy to flow out.

There are several crystals to choose from, and each has its own benefits. I don't want to overwhelm you with all the details; therefore, I am going to share the necessary information with you that you will need to incorporate crystals into your healing journey.

To start, how do you use crystals? Crystal use isn't complicated unless you make it be. You can wear them as jewelry, carry them in your pocket, sleep with them under your pillow, place them around the house or your car, and more.

For the crystals that I am about to share with you, the care for them is simple. Let's explore how to care and use them.

Cleansing your crystals is necessary because they absorb, transform energy and vibrations around them. The beautiful thing about them is they can turn negative energy that they consume into positive energy. You can cleanse them with water, place them outside under the sun or moon, submerge in salt for a day or two, smudge with sage, or use incense. However, should you choose to purchase other crystals, you will want to research crystal care to ensure you don't inadvertently damage it.

Crystals need charging to gain power, just like a phone battery. Sunlight, moonlight, and higher vibrations from other crystals such as selenite, quartz, carnelian, amethyst, and kyanite can charge other crystals. These five crystals are also ones that do not need clearing of negative energy, but they are potent stones to clear other crystals from negative energy and recharge them for use.

When it comes to using crystals to accompany and support your grief journey, there are a few that I recommend. Each of these crystals I have used for my own healing journey and can attest to their unique properties. Let's explore each of these crystals and their specific benefits to support your healing from grief.

Amethyst

Amethyst relieves physical, emotional, and psychological pain or stress. It also eases headaches, releases tension, reduces insomnia and promotes a better night's rest.[1]

Angelite

Angelite helps you speak your truth, be more compassionate, and accepting of things you cannot change. It stimulates healing, eases emotional pain, and creates feelings of peace and tranquility. Spiritually this crystal can help you connect with your angels.[1]

Apache Tear

Apache tear is a form of black obsidian and has its name because it is believed to shed tears in times of sorrow. Therefore it offers comfort during grief, and provides insight into the cause of distress, relieves grievances, and promotes forgiveness.[1]

Black Onyx

Black onyx provides strength and support during difficult times or confusing situations, especially when dealing with mental, emotional, or physical stress. It alleviates overwhelm, fear, and worry.[1]

Clear Quartz

Clear quartz is a master healer and can be used for any condition or situation and is also an amplifier stone. Meaning, it can amplify the energy of other stones.[1]

Howlite

Howlite is a stone that teaches patience and helps to calm turbulent emotions, eliminate rage, pain and stress. It's also an excellent stone for helping with insomnia and meditation because it helps to still the mind.[1]

Kyanite

Kyanite also helps you speak your truth, cut through fear, and blockages. It encourages self-expression and communication. Dispels illusion, anger, frustration, and stress as well.[1]

Malachite

Malachite supports your transformation by drawing out deep feelings and psychosomatic causes, breaks unwanted ties, outdated patterns, and to take responsibility for your actions.[1]

Moonstone

Moonstone is known as the "stone of new beginnings". It calms overreactions to situations and emotional triggers as well as opens the mind to sudden irrational impulse, serendipity, and synchronicity. It soothes emotional instability and stress and stabilizes the emotions.[1]

Rhodonite

Rhodonite heals emotional shock and panic as well as clears away emotional wounds or scars from the past, and promotes forgiveness.[1]

Rose Quartz

Rose quartz strengths empathy, and sensitivity and aids in the acceptance of change. Emotionally it helps to release emotions and heartache as well as soothes the internal pain from grief.[1]

Tiger's Eye

Tiger's eye is helpful for problem solving and resolving internal conflicts, grounding, and aides in healing mental or personality disorders.[1]

You can find crystals through local businesses such as rock or crystals shops, metaphysical or spiritual stores, or several online retailers. However, be careful about purchasing your stones from random retailers. Some sell fake crystals or grow them in labs. They will not have the same energy properties as those sourced from the Earth.

I encourage you to choose a handful of these crystals to try to aid in supporting your healing journey. The five I recommend to start with are amethyst, apache tear, clear and rose quartz, and tiger's eye to assist you during this difficult time.

Chapter 12

Energy Healing

E nergy healing is the final alternative and holistic method to healing from the grief that I am providing you. In this chapter, we are going to briefly discuss energy healing, where I will give a general overview. Energy healing is a broad topic and requires a separate book for itself. Therefore, I am not providing you with a 'how-to' approach to energy healing in this chapter as receiving energy healing treatments requires specific training and should be administered by a certified holistic healing practitioner, like myself.

What is energy healing? Energy healing therapy aims to create a state of peace, balance, and optimum health in a person to remove any energy blockages or imbalances that lead to ailments that impact your mind, body, soul, and spirit. This form of holistic healing works on every level of your life - emotionally, mentally, physically, and spiritually.

Skeptics continually ask if energy healing works. Yes, it does! There are over sixty hospitals worldwide that offer energy healing as part of their alternative treatment options. A study done in 2013 found that 10 minutes of energy healing was as effective as physical therapy in improving the range of motion in people with mobility problems.[1]

There are several benefits for receiving energy healing, some of the reported benefits are as follows:

- Generates overall peace and happiness
- Aids in releasing harmful addictions and habits
- Relaxes the mind and body
- Establishes calmness and balance
- Improves mental clarity and concentration
- Releases negative emotions and thoughts
- Relieves stress, anxiety, and depression
- Dissolves energy blockages
- Improves increases energy
- Strengths self-esteem and confidence
- Clears away built-up toxins
- Reduces fatigue and improves sleep
- Restores your health and strengthens the immune system
- Eases stiffness, pain, tension, and discomfort
- Increases injury recovery rate
- Balances the heart rate, blood pressure, and cortisol
- Assists in reducing or eliminating the chronic problem
- Promotes better digestion

Furthermore, there are a variety of different energy healing modalities. Some of them include Reiki (ray-key), Angelic healing, Crystal healing, Emotional Freedom Techniques® (EFT), Pranic healing, Restorative Touch™, and Quantum Touch®, to name a few.

I specifically want to discuss how grief impacts your body and its chakras and why energy healing is a powerful therapy to use not only when you're grieving, but regularly to maintain optimal wellbeing.

To start, there are four components of grief. They are emotional, mental, physical, and spiritual. Historically, we are taught to use our heads to deal or cope with sorrow rather than our hearts. Unfortunately, this isn't helpful because your heart is the most impacted by a loss.

90

Emotional

When we take a look at the emotional component of grief, it's necessary to understand that it's how your heart reacts to the pain. Since grief is a very emotional reaction to loss, it impacts the heart the most. Emotions are the foundation to support your grief, but also to allow others to try and understand what you, the bereaved, are going through. By not accepting these emotions or feelings, it may become challenging to cope effectively and healthily with your grief.

Mental

The mental component of grief is how your mind responds and reacts to the loss. When we consider the mental aspect of the loss, we are considering the psychological impacts it has on you as a whole. Often this can be seen as mood disorders, such as anxiety or depression, or as shock and guilt, to name a few. The mental component is linked to the emotions and can cause inner turmoil and a domino effect of physical ailments if not addressed quickly or adequately.

Physical

As we look at the physical component of grief, it's necessary to understand that the emotional and mental components of the pain play a part in how your body reacts to the loss. This is part of the domino effect I mentioned previously. The body reacts to grief often by crying and emitting stress hormones that weaken the immune system. The weakened immune system hurts the physical body's ability to resist disease, and as a result, the bereaved become susceptible to illnesses. Some illnesses could include headaches, loss of appetite, weight gain, increased blood pressure, physical pain, and more. By not addressing the physical aspects of grief, your body may not have the energy and endurance to move through the stages of grief healthily.

Spiritual

With the spiritual component of grief, it impacts how the spiritual side of you and your beliefs react to the loss. These impacts could lead to you questioning your religious beliefs or having both negative and positive thoughts about God, death, and the afterlife. It can also trigger you to question things about your life, its purpose, or the meaning of life in general. By not addressing and understanding how your grief impacts your spirit and soul, you cannot know how it affects your spiritual beliefs, which may cause you to miss a crucial aspect for your healing journey.

As you can see, each component builds upon the other and is a domino effect in terms of your whole health and well-being, which is why it's essential to treat yourself whole-istically. By treating only one component of grief, you are essentially throwing a band-aid on it and hoping it'll heal the problem. The fact of the matter is, it won't. You will not see progress with your healing journey if you don't address the root of the problem and how it impacts you emotionally, mentally, physically, and spiritually.

Now that you understand how grief can impact you as a whole, it's necessary to learn how energy healing supports your healing journey. To start, thinking in terms of quantum physics, we know that atoms are spinning and vibrating vortices of energy. Since everything is made up of atoms, everything also has energy. Therefore, we, too, are components of energy, frequency, and vibration.

There are several forms of energy. Some of them include chemical, electromagnetic (light), kinetic (motion), nuclear, thermal, and radiant energies. If we were to use electromagnetic energy as an example, light has different colors of energy because of the various wavelengths. Red has the longest and slowest wavelength, whereas violet has the shortest and fastest wavelength.

Interestingly, color plays a vital role in our lives too. They can impact us both negatively and positively as a whole, especially when considering the four components of grief - emotional, mental, physical, and spiritual. As an example, one person may feel deeper feelings of love when wearing the color red, and another could feel anger. Each person is different and how these colors play a role in their lives and how it impacts them.

We must understand and accept that energy is all around us and part of our daily lives. Therefore, when we utilize energy healing to support our grief, we are tapping into the energy around us to help us stay balanced, aligned, and support our healing journey.

Furthermore, energy healing does not have to be performed in-person; it can be done at a distance. However, never without consent unless there are circumstances that prevent them from providing permission to receive healing. Such as they're a child, medical reasons or they're nearing their end of life, for example.

How does distance energy healing work? In short, quantum physics. Energy healing can be sent via thought, emotion, and intention to the recipient stretching beyond the limits of time and space and sends healing energy healing to reach you no matter where you are. This also means you are not being touched, adjusted, or manipulated physically. The healing session is performed via an exchange of energy between the healer, who is a conduit for the healing from their higher source, and the recipient.

As mentioned previously, there are several forms of energy healing available. I want to encourage you to do your research to determine which would be a good option for you and your unique needs. With that said, I do want to inform you that as a certified energy healing practitioner, I can offer some professional guidance and wisdom to support your decision.

When performing energy healing services for my clients, I combine several modalities with a Christian focus (prayer and meditation) to pack a powerful punch to the healing session. Those energy healing modalities that I combine are Advanced Angelic and Crystal healing, and Usui Reiki. I also include aromatherapy, chromotherapy (color), sound therapy, and forms of divination too.

If we consider energy healing only, for the time being, we want to take note that the end result is the same - unblock and balance chakras or energy centers. There are seven main chakras throughout our bodies. Chakra means "wheel" as an Indian Sanskrit word. These "wheels" have a circular shape that represents a spectrum of colors and is located along the spine. Each chakra has a specific color associated with it, along with particular qualities and energies. They must work together for you to feel your best and have optimal health. When the chakras are blocked or unbalanced, the result can lead to several ailments throughout your body.

Let's explore each chakra a little bit more in-depth so you can have a basic understanding of how they play a role in your healing journey.

Root Chakra (1st)[2][3]

The root chakra is associated with the element Earth and vibrates with the color red. It's located at the base of the spine and includes the legs, feet, bones, large intestine, teeth, and adrenal glands. The purpose of this chakra is grounding, stability, survival, endurance, passion, courage, and individuality. It corresponds to your physical identity and is also the host to fear when the chakra is not in alignment.

When this chakra is out of alignment, some of the physical manifestations include your body feeling heavy or sluggish, sciatica pain, weight issues, or even constipation. You may also feel mentally scattered, ungrounded, or have a deep attachment to feeling secure, usually as a result of fear.

Sacral Chakra (2nd)[2][4]

The sacral chakra is associated with the element water and vibrates with the color orange. It's located just above the pubic bone but below your belly button and includes the hips, low back, groins, sexual organs, womb, kidney, bladder, and circulatory system. The purpose of the sacral chakra is movement or flow, desire, pleasure, sexuality, procreation, sensitivity, feelings, confidence, enthusiasm, joy, and your inner child. It corresponds to your emotional identity, and guilt is often a result of the chakra being out of alignment.

When the sacral chakra is out of alignment, some of the ailments you may experience are impotence, bladder, kidney or uterine trouble, mental issues, and lower back pain. You may also feel over-emotional or numb, careless, or promiscuous, to name a few.

Solar Plexus Chakra (3rd)[2][5]

The solar plexus chakra is associated with the element fire and vibrates with the color yellow. It's located above the belly button but below your heart and includes the upper abdomen, gallbladder, liver, small intestine, stomach, muscles, pancreas, and adrenals. The purpose of this chakra is willpower and ego, assertiveness, laughter or humor, optimism, curiosity, learning, and comprehension. It corresponds to your ego identity, and shame is a result of the solar plexus being out of alignment.

When the solar plexus is not in alignment, you may experience some of the following ailments: ulcers, diabetes, hypoglycemia, digestive issues, or food allergies.

Heart Chakra (4th)[2][6]

The heart chakra is associated with the element air and vibrates with the color green. It's located in the middle of your chest at your heart and includes the heart, ribs, blood, circulatory system, lungs, thymus, breasts, arms, and hands. The purpose of the heart chakra is love, intimacy, balance, relationships, compassion, forgiveness, peace, and harmony, giving without conditions. It corresponds to your social identity, and the demon, the result of an unbalanced chakra, is grief.

95

When this chakra is not in alignment, some of the ailments you may experience are asthma, respiratory issues, high blood pressure, heart or lung disease. You may also experience codependency, the need to meddle or desire for attention, feel judgmental, or isolate yourself.

Throat Chakra (5th)[2][7]

The throat chakra is associated with the element sound and vibrates with the color blue. It's located at your throat and includes neck, mouth, ears, shoulders, thyroid, parathyroid, trachea, cervical vertebrae, vocal cords, and esophagus. The purpose of the throat chakra is communication, creativity, trust, and wisdom. It corresponds with the creative identity, and its reaction to an unbalanced chakra is lies.

When the throat chakra is out of alignment, some ailments may include thyroid issues, speak loudly or scattered, talk too much, or may even be shy or have difficulty speaking.

Third-Eye Chakra (6th)[2][8]

The third-eye chakra is associated with the element light and vibrates with the color indigo. It's located in the middle of your forehead and includes your eyes, nose, sinuses, pineal gland, pituitary gland, and central nervous system. The purpose of this chakra is intuition, insight, vision, imagination, understanding, fearlessness, release, and memory. It corresponds with the archetypal identity, and the adverse reaction to imbalance is an illusion.

When this chakra is not in alignment, some of the ailments may include headaches, poor eyesight, earaches, and nightmares.

Crown Chakra (7th)[2][9]

The crown chakra is associated with the element consciousness and vibrates with the color violet (or white). It's located at the top or crown of your head and includes the head, brain, skin, central nervous system. The purpose of this chakra is spirituality, bliss, wisdom, understanding, awareness, higher self, charisma, awakening, and union with the Divine (your source or a higher power - God). It corresponds with the universal identity, and attachment or ignorance is the casualty of the imbalanced chakra.

When the crown chakra is out of balance, some of the ailments you may experience are migraines, tension headaches, depression, confusion, alienation, boredom, apathy, and inability to learn. You may also feel a disconnect from reality and the Divine, be overly concerned with your intellect, be cynical, close-minded, and develop a spiritual addiction.

As we previously discussed, the heart is most impacted by grief. Therefore, the fourth or heart chakra needs the most healing and care. Yes, grief can affect all of the other chakras throwing them out of balance or becoming blocked, but more often than not, the heart chakra is what needs the most attention.

Grief, unfortunately, is an energy-depleting emotion. Therefore it sucks the energy out of you, so to speak. Your body needs the strength to be healthy, and that energy can come from eating a balanced diet, getting exercise, being in nature, listening to music, and more.

If you, as the griever, are not "recharging your batteries" daily, your body is losing energy. As a result, you will not feel your best and, over time, will begin to feel worse. Your body can only endure this much abuse for so long, and once it reaches its breaking point, several ailments ensue, which is why it's not uncommon to see those who are grieving to become ill. It's inevitable when you're putting your body through hell and not caring for it like you should.

Energy healing can support you while grieving because, as a whole, everything is off-kilter. For example, mentally, you may be experiencing anxiety. Emotionally you may feel a sense of shock or anger. Physically you may experience loss of appetite, fatigue, or a feeling of heaviness throughout your body. Spiritually, you may feel lost and alone. All of these are manifestations of the body when your chakras aren't in alignment.

When receiving energy healing, whether you're grieving or not, the goal is to improve or maintain the flow of energy within the body, which will activate the healing process. This energy knows precisely where to go to balance and heal. It's often said that it will give you what you NEED, not what you necessarily WANT.

I must mention that energy healing does not magically take away someone's grief and sadness. It does support the griever to deal with the turbulent ups and downs as they move through each of the nine stages of grief. Being calm and collected supports the griever to process emotions healthily and the energy needed to heal from the loss.

What are the physical benefits of energy healing to support your grief? In short, energy healing helps to increase energy, reduce muscle tension, and clear toxins.

Replenishing your energy and balancing your chakras is vital so that you can get through the day without feeling off-kilter and it makes it easier for your body to fight off any illnesses which can prolong your healing journey.

Additionally, grief can cause physical pain throughout your body, and often the bereaved feel like a ticking time bomb. With the support of energy healing, it reduces muscle tension that is wreaking havoc on your body through tensed shoulders, clenched jaw, headaches, etc. As the pressure builds, it can cause worry and anxiety. When you feel more relaxed, you are better able to cope and handle your grief and support your body through the healing process.

Lastly, your body is continually burning energy to rebuild tissue and replaces older or damaged cells throughout your body. Therefore, your body creates a significant amount of waste (internal toxins) that your body must break down and eliminate. Unfortunately, grief can contribute to the toxins being stuck within your cells, soft tissue, and muscles. Therefore overwhelming your entire immune system causing the body to ineffectively breakdown and eliminate the waste. When these toxins build up, they leave you more susceptible to illness. Energy healing can support your body to clear the toxins allowing you to stay healthy.

As you can see, energy healing goes hand in hand with supporting those suffering from grief. The benefits, in my opinion, are invaluable, and I highly recommend energy healing for anyone no matter their age or circumstance because I have felt and experienced its power and healing, and so should you.

Part 4

Transformation

"Grief is the nasty game of feeling the weakest you have ever felt and morphing it into the strongest person you will have to become."

- Windgate Lane

Chapter 13

Pain Into Purpose

―――――――――――― ∾∾∾∾∾ ――――――――――――

No matter what type of challenging circumstance you face in your life, you can overcome it. In fact, you can even transform the pain into a purpose!

Josh Shipp, an American youth motivational speaker, best-selling author, and TV personality, says, "You can either get bitter, or you get better. It's that simple. You take what has been dealt to you and allow it to make you a better person, or you allow it to tear you down. The choice does not belong to fate; it belongs to you."

Harsh but powerful and accurate.

Most likely, you have a painful memory from your past - heartbreak or disappointment, a traumatic event, abuse, violence, and even old anger that's accumulated over the years. It's necessary to move forward, to forgive, let go, and live in the present moment. However, too many, those words seem daunting.

Understand this - true freedom comes from accepting what has happened to you and using the pain to make a difference.

Hindsight is 20/20; therefore, when you reflect on the challenging times in your life and feel gratitude instead of bitterness, resentment, or anger, you fully understand that it was all part of God's plan, a catalyst for your growth.

Learning to turn your sorrow into meaning dissolves negative emotions and replaces it with happiness and a renewed love for life. Truthfully, there is no better way to channel the pain and pull yourself or a loved one out of the depths of hell than by taking the lead and guiding them out of misery.

I feel it's important to remind you that grief is a journey, and it will be unique to you, and it is not linear. When you're ready to transform your pain into a purpose, there are a series of steps one needs to take to work through their grief and heal from it.

Chapter 14

Finding Clarity

To find clarity around the pain from losing your loved one, I would like to invite you to grab a notebook, journal, or refer to the journal pages at the end of the book and a pen. It's time to delve deeper into the pain and reflect on the situation so that you can move forward with your healing journey.

Take a few moments to ground and balance yourself by saying a prayer and engaging in mindful meditation. You want to begin this exercise with a fresh mind and balanced emotions. Once you are ready to proceed, think back to the loss of your loved one and capture as many memories that you can recall - both good and bad. This will help your healing process as well as support you in finding clarity around your purpose.

Using bullet points to organize your thoughts is one idea or verbally tell your story and write it down in your journal. Write down anything that comes to mind. Don't worry about the order of events or fussing about proper grammar and punctuation. You can do this later, but for now, let the flow of your thoughts and your heart fill the paper without judgment, fear, or self-doubt. When done, organize your memories and experiences into chronological order.

Next, create a list of your God-given gifts, skills, experience, and passions.

Determine what sparks joy and makes you happy. Would you enjoy organizing events, writing a book, speaking, teaching, volunteering, or something different altogether? Knowing this information will help you later with transforming your pain; therefore, you must identify what brings you happiness despite the pain.

Once you have outlined what brings you joy, it's time to review your journal notes. Here you will want to look for anything that stands out to you as significant or essential, evaluate if you can see an underlying theme or pattern, or identify what sets your soul on fire.

For example, let's say one of your God-given skills is the ability to paint beautiful watercolor art. It brings you joy, and your loved one also had a flair for the arts; therefore, it was a shared bond between the two of you. As such, this could be the foundation for your project.

Keep in mind, you may find this easy or difficult, but either way, show yourself some grace. If you're struggling to find the pattern or more profound meaning, take a step back, wait a few hours, a day or two, and review your notes again. Please don't get discouraged. If you are still having trouble, ask a loved one to be a sounding board. You will find what you're looking for, I promise, and this will become the basis for your Pain to Purpose Project.

As you embark on your Pain to Purpose Project, I encourage you to embrace the unknown and learn to trust yourself while on this healing journey. There will be moments where you feel doubt and second guess yourself that you're doing the right thing when nothing seems to be working in your favor. However, no matter what - tune into your internal GPS and stay on the road to your final destination. Do not give up! Faith over fear, my friend.

Chapter 15

Creating a Movement

N ow that you have identified the initiative of your Pain to Purpose Project, it's time to create a movement! A movement is about organizing people together because of a shared purpose.

As with the last exercise, get some paper, or use the journal pages at the end of the book and fetch a pen, let's dive in and create your movement. Spend some time writing in your journal the following questions:

1. What changes do you want to make that'll have an impact locally, nationally, or globally?
2. What people do you want to bring together with the movement?
3. What specifically about your loved one inspires this movement?
4. What benefits would this movement bring to the people you are bringing together?
5. What, individually, do you stand for and believe in that lights a fire deep inside of you?
6. Why will others rally around your movement - your big "why"?
7. What would potentially "ruffle the feathers" or provoke discussion about your movement?
8. What is your mission and vision for this movement?
9. Who can you connect with that would get on board and support your movement and influence others?

10. What do others need to do to be part of your movement, or how can they get involved?

Now that you delved deeper into your pain and finding your purpose through creating a movement that will honor your loved one, it's time to connect the dots by determining how you can utilize your skills that will bring you joy.

For example, we previously mentioned that you are a skilled watercolor artist. Your loved one also was an art enthusiast and passionate about animals. A plausible Pain to Purpose Project could be using your art to create awareness for animal rights.

Take another few minutes to write down any additional thoughts about the movement, as this will help you later on when we tie everything together for your Pain to Purpose Project. When done, let's explore how you plan to share your movement with others.

Chapter 16

Getting Innovative

L ook at you! You're moving right along. So far, you found clarity surrounding your pain and explored your passions and created the foundation for a movement that will honor your loved one. Next up is letting your creativity run wild and determine how you plan to share your message with the masses!

Again, grab a pen, some paper, or refer to the journal pages at the back of the book, as we have some more work to do. Consider your skills and passions, the memory of your loved one, and make a list of all how you could advocate for your movement. I have outlined a few questions to help spark some ideas to get your creative juices flowing, see below.

1. What viable options are already in place that is similar to the movement that I could use as inspiration?
2. Of the viable options, how could I make them bigger, better, or fill the gap?
3. What's the most comfortable or most straightforward way I can use my gifts and honor my loved one?
4. If time or money weren't an issue, what would be the most grandeur way I could honor my loved one with my gifts and passions?
5. How much time, money, and energy, am I willing to put into this movement?
6. What options make the most sense to my movement and the people

I intend to gather for the cause?

7. What can I do differently to stand out from the crowd to create a successful movement?

Once you are done with writing down your innovative ideas to share your message, you'll want to take a few moments to organize your thoughts further to connect the dots.

For example, let's continue to use our example that you are a skilled watercolor artist, and your loved one was an art enthusiast too, and passionate about animals. As mentioned, a plausible movement is to use your art to create awareness for animal rights.

We can then expand upon this by thinking outside of the box various ways to honor our loved one with our Pain to Purpose Project. Some of the plausible ideas could be the following:

- painting animal portraits for their owners
- selling animal inspired paintings and donating the funds to a reputable charity in memory of your loved one
- creating a children's book using your art for illustrations that teach children about the importance of loving and caring for animals
- creating a non-profit, that focuses on animal rights and use your art to raise money through various fundraising events

With that said, it's important to note that your movement can be small scale or large. Ultimately it's up to you; just know that a small pebble in the water can create a ripple effect too. Trust your intuition and let your heart guide you as you finalize your decision for your Pain to Purpose Project.

Once you have finalized your Pain to Purpose Project, it's now time to consider options for naming it and determining how you plan to share it with others. Take another few minutes to write down possible names for your movement, as this will help you later on when we finish connecting the dots.

Chapter 17

Developing a Strategy

First and foremost, congratulations on making it this far into working through your pain and transforming it into your purpose. I understand this likely wasn't easy for you, but know that as you work through each phase, you are also healing yourself from grief. Your loved one wants you to be happy, and that does not mean you have moved on or forgotten them. You are learning to mend your broken heart, cherish the memories, live with the pain, and honor them. You can and will get through this - one day at a time.

Now that you have officially determined your Pain to Purpose Project, it's time to create a plan of action!

Based on your project and the size of your movement, your action steps will vary in a multitude of ways. Please keep this in mind. For example, if your movement is to make a regular donation to a charity in honor of your loved one, then your plan of action is simple - choose the charity and make the donation. However, if your movement is grandeur, and you are creating a non-profit organization, then your steps will be a lot more in-depth and require a more strategic approach.

As such, get a pen, some paper, or refer to the end of the book for journal pages, so you can outline your strategy!

To start, dump all of your ideas or action steps onto your paper. Don't worry about organizing them at this point or being in chronological order; the goal is just to get everything out of your head onto paper.

Here are some questions to help facilitate this process.

1. What do I know that will aid the project overall?
2. What don't I know or need to do more research about for the project?
3. What type of outside support do I need to see this project come to life?
4. What do I need to be legally compliant?
5. Who do I know that I can enlist to support me with my Pain to Purpose Project?
6. How will I share the message of my Pain to Purpose Project with others?
7. What, if any, upfront expenses are needed? On average, how much?

Next, perform the necessary research to bring your project to fruition. Continue to add to your list any additional steps and making notes as you see fit that is generated from your research.

When done, it's time to organize the steps into chronological order. For me, I like to group them into sections or main tasks and then create subtasks. I love the visual, and it's a good reminder to "eat an elephant: a bite at a time."

If you're like me and thrive off of electronic organization, then I recommend that you use a free project management tool, like Asana or Trello. If you're old school, that's cool too, simply organize your notes, so they're in chronological order.

Review your plan of action one last time to determine if there's anything you have forgotten. If nothing comes to mind, let's move onto execution!

Chapter 18

Executing the Strategy

N ow that you have found clarity, created a movement, got innovative, and developed the strategy, it's time to execute it!

I find that many people get hung up on the execution piece of a strategy. Lucky for you, my top strengths, according to the CliftonStrengths (formerly Clifton *StrengthsFinder),* are strategic, ideation, learner, input, and achiever. What does that mean? The first four are all categorized as strategic thinking, and the fifth is executing or execution. Therefore, not only can I provide you one uniquely creative strategy, I can help you implement it!

Since you have your strategy and it's in chronological order, it's time to create deadlines to see this dream come to fruition. If you are using an electronic project management system, which is what I recommend, you can select due dates for the first set of tasks to complete. If you are going old school, purchase an inexpensive calendar or print off blank calendar sheets and pencil in tasks to assign deadlines.

Things to consider are when you can start on the project, how many tasks you can complete in a week and when, and the date in which you want to see the project go live. Once you have a general idea of the timeline, you can start setting deadline dates to hold yourself accountable.

A suggestion is to break it down so it doesn't become overwhelming. For example, if the project has a goal for completion in one year, I would break it down into quarterly goals, the monthly focused topics, weekly tasks, and daily priority to-dos.

The more you can break down the larger tasks into smaller ones, the more accomplished you will feel as you check them off the list, but the less overwhelmed you will feel. Which means you are less likely to procrastinate or throw in the towel altogether.

Once you have your deadlines set, it's essential to determine how you plan to celebrate the milestones as you strive to finalize your Pain to Purpose Project. No matter if it's big or small, we love them all! These celebrations could be having a treat you usually don't allow yourself to have, buying yourself a little extra something from your favorite store, a trip to the spa, etc. Celebrating the milestones is a way to keep you motivated, inspired, and to keep the good vibes coming - it's an abundance thing!

Lastly, I want to remind you to show yourself some grace while you work on your Pain to Purpose Project. I can tell you first hand that this will stir up emotions, both good and bad. It will challenge you, push you out of your comfort zone, and maybe even make you want to give up.

Please know it's all part of the healing process. Your pain, unfortunately, will never go away, it may lessen over time, but it'll always be there, and so too will the memories that will trigger you when you least expect it. You are healing from grief one day at a time, don't expect yourself to be *perfect*, but choose to go with the flow and embrace this new normal.

Chapter 19

My Pain to Purpose Project

—————————— ❧ ——————————

I feel it's only fair and fitting to share with you my Pain to Purpose Project so that you can see this process come full circle and help you tie everything together that you just learned. To start, my Pain to Purpose Project is called the Dale J Paulin Memorial Fund.

As you know, I lost my father to cancer. What you may not know is that it was a service-connected illness he received after courageously and selflessly serving our country during the Vietnam War.

After his passing, I felt a longing in my heart to make a difference in the lives of other military families no matter their current status with the military but wasn't 100% sure what God was calling me to do.

Until one day, during prayer and meditation, I received a *divine download*. At that moment, with my eyes closed, a movie played in my mind's eye, and it's where God revealed my calling.

To subtly say I became *woke* is an understatement.

Harnessed with the divine vision, a passion for serving others, and a Godly mission to complete, I embarked on a transformative journey that led me to fulfill my life's purpose.

While accompanying my father to various doctor's appointments, treatments, and surgeries, I noticed a gap in his care plan. While he had an incredible team of professionals through the Veterans Administration (VA) Hospital, none promoted or advocated for any holistic or alternative services. Had I known what I know now, my father's care plan would have looked a little bit differently.

As a way to honor my late father, the Dale J Paulin Memorial Fund was created.

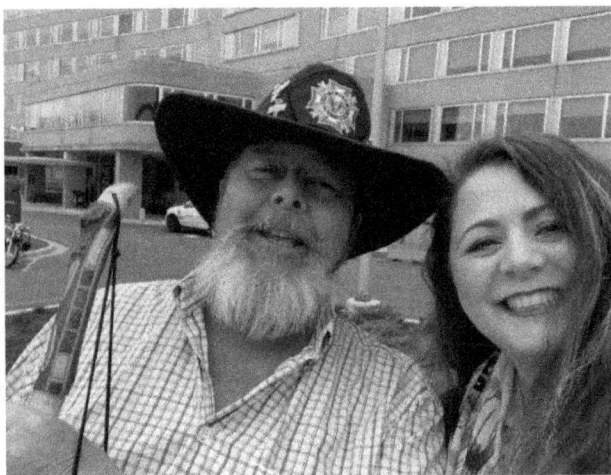

This fund will provide free life coaching and alternative and holistic services to servicemen and women to support them on their healing journey.

There are three incredible ways you can make a difference and support me and my mission:

Make a Purchase

When you purchase any services from the Intuitive Spiritual Warrior Holistic Healing & Consulting™, a portion of the sale will go directly to the fund and get used accordingly to support a service member.

Sponsor a Service

When you choose to sponsor a service, you will select the type of service you wish to donate to a service member and pay the appropriate fee. Your sponsorship can be completely anonymous, or if you desire, your name will get passed onto the recipient. You will receive notification of its redemption.

Give a Monetary Donation

When you decide to give a monetary donation, it'll go directly to the fund and get used accordingly to support a service member. Your sponsorship can be completely anonymous, or if you desire, your name will get passed onto the recipient. You will receive notification of its redemption.

If interested, you can make a donation here: intuitivespiritualwarrior.com/donate

You see, God placed a colossal dream on my heart, and this fund is only the beginning. It's both exhilarating and intimidating to know the mission he bestowed upon me to complete. The saying goes, "God doesn't call the qualified; He qualifies the called." I truly believe this! Every day I remind myself that I am answering the call, and that keeps me inspired to pursue this mission and complete my Pain to Purpose Project.

Lastly, as a side note, if you are an alternative or holistic healing practitioner and would like to discuss ways in which you can support my mission and partner with me to provide various services to members of the United States military, please connect with me at kayla@intuitivespiritualwarrior.com.

Part 5

Wrap-up

"The reality is that you will grieve forever. You will not 'get over' the loss of a loved one; you will learn to live with it. You will heal and you will rebuild yourself around the loss you have suffered. You will be whole again but you will never be the same. Nor should you be the same nor would you want to."

- Elisabeth Kubler-Ross

Chapter 20

Final Thoughts on Grief & Loss

A s we come to the closing of this book, I hope you enjoyed the content and found value in what I shared with you about the various ways to heal from grief.

Remember that grief and mourning can last months or even years, and the pain is eased as time passes. Eventually, the grieving will lessen, and you will adapt to life without your loved one, and you will begin to pick up the pieces of your life.

I want to leave you with some final thoughts about grief and your healing journey.

- Accept this new life transition without your loved one by embracing your new normal.
- Understand that the topic of death, loss, and grief is uncomfortable and awkward for most people to experience, discuss, or even the uncertainty of support to offer.
- Enjoy life as much as possible, make new friends, continue or start new hobbies, take up new interests, or start a new project.
- Embrace and feel the pain and rollercoaster of emotions as they come, don't push them aside.
- Express your feelings honestly, freely, and respectfully as it will

allow you to process the grief and assist others in knowing how to best support you during this challenging life transition.

- Take care of yourself - mind, body, soul, and spirit to support the transformation you are experiencing.
- Turn to your loved ones for help, and do not feel ashamed about it.
- Lean into your faith and build a relationship with God or your higher power.
- Seek support for grief and loss either privately or in a group with a professional.

Lastly, I am in the trenches with you. I know the pain you are experiencing. If I can be of assistance in any way, please do not hesitate to connect with me. You will find my contact information at the back of the book in my author bio.

May you continue to heal, find your inner peace, and transform your life. May God watch over you and grant you peace.

Chapter 21

Additional Exercises to Support Grief

———————— ❦ ————————

There are several exercises that you can do to support your healing journey. If you were to do an Internet search or browse Pinterest, you would find thousands of options available for you to pick and choose from. I welcome you to do that if your heart desires, but I will share with you some of my favorite exercises that either myself or my clients have used to support their healing journey. Let's take a look!

Art Therapy

A common misconception is that you have to be creative or an artist to utilize art therapy. In short, that simply isn't true. The goal is to find alternative ways to support your healing journey, and art therapy provides a creative outlet. More often than not, when those mourning a loss engage in art therapy, they find it easier to work through their emotions and have a better understanding of them. It allows them to use different parts of their brain and see things from a different perspective.

There are several benefits to art therapy. Some of these benefits include:

- Relieving stress
- Boosting self-esteem
- Increasing empathy and dopamine

- Encouraging creativity
- Assisting in becoming more self-aware
- Supporting becoming more psychologically resilient
- Improving memory
- Supporting creative expression of feelings

Some simple ideas for art therapy include doodling in a journal, creating or printing a mandala to color, or creating past and future hearts. The past and future hearts are a fun and simple exercise that anyone can do, no matter their artistic skill level.

Whether you want to draw two hearts on a piece of paper, cut two out of construction paper, or print the illustration from bonus materials on my website, the choice is yours. Get creative with this exercise. You can use crayons, colored pencils, markers, paint, chalk, or whatever you feel called to use. All you need is two hearts to represent your past and your future. You may also need a piece of paper to write down some notes for each heart, but from there, you can design your hearts.

For the heart that will represent your past, ask yourself the following questions:

- What words come to mind when I think about my past and the loss of my loved one?
- What imagery reflects my past?
- What feelings and emotions reflect my past?
- What colors reflect my past?
- Who was I in my past?

For the heart that will represent your future, ask yourself the following questions:

- What words do I want to reflect on my future self once I am healed?
- What imagery do I want to reflect on my future self?

- What feelings and emotions do I want to have in the future?
- What colors do I want to reflect on my future?
- Who do I want to be or become in the future?

As you look at your two completed hearts, reflect on your healing journey. You know where you started, and you now have a creative mental picture of where you want to be. Use it as inspiration and to instill hope when you feel like you may be back-peddling versus moving forward with your healing journey.

Remember, practice makes progress, not perfection. Moving forward, even if it's baby steps, is more important than sitting at a standstill. Keep that in mind as you continue on this healing journey.

Bereavement Box

A bereavement (or memory) box is a beautiful way to honor your loved one's memory by gathering and storing their favorite items or anything that reminds you of them. This could be in a shadow box you display on the wall, a trinket box, a simple decorative box you can find at your local craft store, or if you're crafty, you could hand-make one with wood and paint it. Don't overcomplicate it.

The box should be unique to you and your loved one. You may write or carve their name on it, choose to include dates, nicknames, or other relevant information that has meaning between you and your loved one.

Some tangible items you could place within the box are as follows:

- Favorite article of clothing
- Favorite books
- Letters, cards, or journal
- Keychain
- Jewelry

- Photos
- Awards or certificates
- Medals or pendants
- Newspaper articles
- Other memorabilia

This isn't an all-encompassing list, but you get a general idea. Refer to the box when you are missing your loved one and need to feel closer to them in spirit. The items will provide you some peace and comfort while you weather the storm.

Bible Study

As strange as this may be to see Bible study as an additional healing exercise, it's really a powerful way to strengthen your faith during this challenging time and either renew, improve, or further strengthen your relationship with God.

If you have never studied the Bible, don't worry, you can learn just as I did. There are three necessary steps to Bible Study; observe, interpret, and apply.

1. Observe

   - What does the scripture say?
   - How is it said?
   - What terminology are you unfamiliar with that you need to research in the dictionary and thesaurus?
   - What words or phrases stand out to you?
   - What are your initial thoughts about the scripture verse?

2. Interpret

   - What does the scripture mean?
   - What's the context?
   - What other versions of the Bible can you use to cross-

reference the scripture?

- What's your interpretation of the scripture?
- Are they similar or different? How so?

3. Apply

- What can I do to apply the scripture to my life?
- What's the true meaning of the scripture, and how does it impact my relationship with God?
- How does the truth affect the relationship I have with others?
- How does the truth affect me emotionally, mentally, and spiritually?
- How does this truth impact my response to reject sin, the enemy, etc.?

For 10-15 minutes a day, read or listen to the word of God. Write the scripture into a journey, study it, record your findings, and reflect. Below are some scripture verses to help get you started. *(Note: The scripture is from the New International Version (NIV))*

- Isaiah 40:28-31
- Psalms 16:7-11
- Lamentations 3:31-33
- Matthew 5:4
- John 14:1-4

- Romans 8:16-18
- 1 Corinthians 15: 51-57
- 2 Corinthians 1:3-7
- 1 Peter 1:3-9
- Revelation 21:3-4

Feelings Wheel

The feelings wheel is a simple way to acknowledge how you're feeling and explore how to manage negative emotions. You will need paper and a pen for this exercise.

1. Create a circle on the paper.
2. Split the circle, like a pizza, in eight slices or sections.
3. Write one word in each of the sections: angry, anxiousness, fear

guilt, hopelessness, loneliness, sadness, worry.

Once you have your wheel created, choose one place to start, and review each emotion. Ask yourself the following questions for each emotion and write the responses in the corresponding section.

- What are my initial thoughts about this emotion in my current state?
- How does this emotion make me feel?
- How does my body feel when I am experiencing this emotion?
- What happened today (or recently) that prompted me to feel this emotion?
- Did I process this emotion in a healthy or unhealthy way?
- How can I do better to manage this emotion going forward?

Grief Strategy

Grieving the loss of your loved one is one of the most difficult challenges you will face throughout your lifetime. Over time, you will mend your broken heart and learn to live life without them. However, there will be periods where you succumb to the emotions of grief, and one of the different ways to prepare for those moments is with a grief strategy. Not only will it help you with having to make difficult decisions while you're not yourself, but it'll also help your family members to support you while you are in this state.

Your Grief Strategy helps you identify helpful ways to cope with your feelings of loss, set healthy boundaries, and create a way to work through and feel the emotions that are for your highest good.

All you need for this exercise is paper and a pen. Read through each question, reflect, and write down your thoughts. This will help you to create and finalize your Grief Strategy. I encourage you to keep it readily available so that both you and your loved ones have access to it when it's needed the most.

- When I feel angry, what can I do to help me cope with my feelings of grief and loss?
- When I feel anxious or worried, what can I do to help me cope with my feelings of grief and loss?
- When I feel sad or depressed, what can I do to help me cope with my feelings of grief and loss?
- When I feel scared, what can I do to help me cope with my feelings of grief and loss?
- Who can I talk to that will help me feel better?
- Who can I lean on for support to help me cope?
- What positive thoughts can I think and reflect on during these challenging times?
- What affirmations can I read to myself to provide me hope and inspiration to help me cope?
- What am I committed to doing to take care of myself during these moments when I'm struggling to cope?
- What healthy boundaries do I need in place for my safety when I am unable to cope?
- When should your loved ones call for professional help?
- Who is your support buddy to make a judgment call on your behalf? Should you be unable to cope and need professional help?
- What are the names and numbers of medical professionals?

When done, display it in an area where your loved ones will see it, and so will you as a constant reminder of your plan.

Self-Care

As simple as this one sounds, it's often one of the last things we do for ourselves when mourning the loss of a loved one. I include it here as an additional exercise as a reminder that this, too, will help with your healing. Be consistent, and you will reap the rewards for your efforts.

Options for self-care include, but are not limited to:

- Eating a well-balanced diet
- Getting at least 30-minutes of exercise daily
- Drinking plenty of water
- Taking a shower or hot bath
- Getting dressed
- Participating in hobbies and other interesting activities
- Getting enough rest

An excellent way to hold yourself accountable for practicing intentional-self-care is to keep a log of the activities you do throughout the day and review them weekly to determine how you can make some necessary changes to maintain your well-being.

Write a Letter

Writing a letter to your loved one is a beautiful way to process your emotions, verbalize what is on your mind, and be therapeutic in nature. As you write the letter, don't worry about grammar and punctuation. Simply write and let it flow.

You could write a letter to tell them about something new in your life, to say hello, apologize, ask a question, share your thoughts, or to say goodbye. The choice is yours. Use pretty stationery, notebook paper, a blank notecard, a journal, or whatever your heart desires. The important thing is to write.

Once you have the letter written, read it out loud, and allow your mind to process the words. When done, you can save it, shred it, or some people like to burn it as more of a symbolic way to carry the message to their loved one in heaven.

Chapter 22

Grief & Bereavement Support

T he following websites contain relevant information pertaining to grief and bereavement. These centers and agencies provide a broad range of programs to people and their communities struggling with grief and loss. Support is closer than you may realize. Within these websites, you will likely find the support and resources you need so that you can continue to live a vibrant and fulfilling life while healing from grief.

Association of Death Education & Counseling (ADEC)[1]

The ADEC has over 2,000+ members and includes mental and physical health practitioners, parents, church members, funeral directors, and more that offer resources pertaining to death education, care of the dying, grief counseling, and research in thanatology.

Center for Loss & Life Transition[2]

The Center for Loss & Life Transition provides support to those who grieve as well as those who loved them to have the right direction to conquer sorrow and lead productive lives while healing from grief. Founded 20+ years ago, their approach advocates for a "companioning" approach to bereavement versus a "treating" approach.

Grief.com[3]

Grief.com provides a plethora of resources and support for those that are grieving or their loved ones who want to support them during this difficult life transition. The online community offers resources that include professional services providers, grief data and support, books, and more to provide support for grief and bereavement.

Grief Resource Network[4]

The Grief Resource Network is a community of those who are grieving and professionals who support them. The network provides both comfort and guidance to those who are suffering from the loss of a loved one as well as resources. Some of these resources include government resources, crisis relief assistance, meetings or events, professional service providers, relevant grief research studies and data, book, and movie recommendations.

Hospice Foundation of America (HFA)[5]

HFA provides resources and trust information on end of life, hospice care, grief, and bereavement for caregivers and their loved ones to find support with this major life transition.

Intuitive Spiritual Warrior Holistic Consulting & Healing™[6]

The Intuitive Spiritual Warrior Holistic Consulting & Healing™ promotes emotional, mental, physical, and spiritual healing through alternative and holistic methods. Offering comfort, guidance, and healing for the mind, body, soul, and spirit.

LJG Candles & Gifts[7]

LJG Candles & Gifts provides memorial gifts for those grieving or their loved ones to offer as a beautiful sympathy gift. The owner, Rachael, handmakes each order to be sure every piece is as unique as your grief.

National Suicide Prevention Lifeline[8]

The National Suicide Prevention Lifeline is a nationwide network providing local crisis centers offering free and confidential emotional support to those in a suicidal crisis or emotional distress 24/7. Their objective is to prevent suicide by empowering individuals, advancing professional best practices, and building awareness.

Dial the National Suicide Prevention Line at 1-800-273-TALK or send a text message to 741741 with TALK for support.

Open to Hope[9]

Open to Hope is a non-profit organization dedicated to helping those grieving to find hope following the loss of a loved one through motivational posts, books, and an online community. Their goal is to give a voice to grief recovery and support people to cope with painful losses so they can continue to live happy, meaningful lives while healing from grief.

Substance Abuse and Mental Health Services Administration (SAMHSA) National Hotline[10]

The SAMSHA is an agency within the U.S. Department of Health and Human Services that offers support and resources pertaining to substance abuse and mental illness to those struggling with addiction or for their loved ones.

Part 6

Bonus Story

Chapter 23

Forever Stamped on My Heart

by Nicki Blucher

A person's journey with cancer affects the whole family. Sure my mother's cancer affected hers in many more ways than I could imagine. I wasn't the one poked with needles, and having tests ran weekly. I didn't lose my hair, nails, and teeth. I didn't lose my ability to have strength in my arms and legs and be bound to a wheelchair. I wasn't the one that would prepare for the end of my life. I can't write about that kind of journey. What I can write about is what it's like to have a mother who battled cancer. I can write about what it is like to tell my mother goodbye and all the in-between moments we had. Cancer has changed me and has become a part of my own journey in life.

The day my mother died will be forever stamped on my heart. We had been at the hospital all day. Unfortunately, this was common at this point of her health so nobody, not even the doctors, expected her to die.

Looking back, I think my mother was the only one who knew she wasn't going to leave the hospital this time. For years I knew cancer would claim my mother's life. She was always so positive and strong, it seemed like that was years off. At that moment, time seemed to have gone so fast.

In my mind, I had to ask myself, how could almost six years of her living with cancer have already passed? How did we get to this moment?

I wasn't ready to say goodbye to the woman who had meant the world to me. She had brought me into this world, and even as a 34-year-old woman, I still needed her. But at the moment she told me she was ready to go, I knew I had to be prepared.

With water filled in the corner of my eyes that slowly streamed down my cheeks, I had blessed her decision. I didn't think twice, it was just that easy to grant her permission to die. It was easy to tell her that she had been amazing, and I was proud of her. There was nothing she could have done better or different, and I was blessed I could tell her that. It was all true, and I still stand by my words.

For everything she had been to me and had done for me, it was easy to let her go. In this lifetime, she was never selfish. I had always come first to her above all her needs, and she wore her love for me on her sleeve every day.

As a child, I was lucky. I never worried about how loved I was. I never worried if I would be cared for. I always knew I had her in my corner no matter what had happened or what decision I had made. So telling my mother she could die, was the only right thing I could do. What I soon would realize is the not easy part would be learning to live in a world where she no longer existed.

I have lost family members before, and I have grieved, but no grief ever felt so deep then losing my mom. When my mom died, a part of me died too. My very existence had changed instantly, and I desperately wanted to feel normal again. I had never felt physical pain from grief before. Never had I found myself slumped over a garbage can puking out raw emotion. I waited for the pain to pass, surly after the funeral, my healing could begin. Once it didn't move, I thought maybe after the first month, even the first year. Now that I am processing through my second year without a mom, I have accepted my pain is still real, and it is now a part of me. I will never wake up and just stop needing and missing my mother. This is the reality of my new life.

I had to accept that grief only exists where love was first. I started thinking of how blessed I was to be loved so much. I had been born into a loving family, and not everyone can say that. My mom always wanted me to celebrate her life and go out and live a life I was meant to live. I think about this daily to keep myself moving forward. Some days are still brutal.

I might appear to have it together, and the right song comes on, and I melt into an ocean of salty tears. The smallest things can bring about a wave of grief. I had to learn to stop looking for the "me" that once was. I had to realize I was forever changed. Life as I knew it didn't exist because my mother didn't. I now live in a world without a mother, and that has left me forever changed. Instead of pushing that change away and being sad and scared to face the days ahead of me, I embraced it. I accepted that this was my story all along. I was to be motherless in the physical world someday, and I can't change that fact.

The days of shedding tears are never over, and I know I will have hard moments ahead of me. My biggest challenge will be being a mother in a motherless world. I still find myself grabbing the phone to tell her the latest news of what my daughters accomplished in school, to invite her to birthdays and school events, and to ask her what was in that recipe the kids loved so much.

I often sob uncontrollably for my daughters, who were left without a grandma in their life. I am blessed to still have mine in my life. She was there for me all through my life and all those milestones - graduations, marriage, and babies being born. I find it heartbreaking my children will not have those moments and memories. I miss all the things I know my girls will need her for.

I always tell them it will be ok to cry and laugh and some days not know how to feel. For my daughters, I stopped feeling like I died inside. I remembered something my mother said to me. She said to look into the mirror, and I would know she is still here. She is right; I am my mother, and I can travel the rest of my journey. My children will need me to, and they will need me now more than ever. Instead of feeling a part of me died inside, I am reminded I am a part of my mother, and that part of her will live on in me. Living is honoring the ones who have passed before us.

It was my mother, who was my greatest supporter. She always believed in me and told me to keep writing. For years I put that dream on the back burner, but it is the living part of me that needs to tell my story. It is my mother's need for me to do what I was meant to do that drives me. It is her memory that reminds me to live the life I was meant to live. Even in her death, she continues to inspire me and change me. Perhaps this is where the journey of the new me begins.

Waves of Wazeecha

In loving memory of Debra Dillman

Warm Air brushes against her face, as her kayak glides over small ripples of water made from the fishermen who pass.

Her visor blocks rays of sunshine that peak above the green canopy of trees that surround her.

A fish jumps, making ringlets on water, distracting her search for the Great Blue Heron.

On the water she finds peace. On the water cancer doesn't exist.

I glance over the water, my shoes pressing against the brown sand of the shore. My mother lived everyday with the possibility of tomorrow.

As I step into her kayak, it rocks over small ripples of water made from the fishermen who pass.

Summer wind brushes softly against my face. It is as if my mother is whispering I love you. It was the last thing I said to her, as I softy released her hand and watched her fade away. It is as if in this moment my soul is connected to her soul once again.

Rays of sunshine touch my skin, and the warmth of childhood memories growing up on these waters surface. I see our tubs being pulled behind the boat, only to fly off landing in cold water. The burn and aches we felt, but we would always go again. I see fishing on the paddle boat and laugh when I remember when my line got tangled with moms. I wonder if the baby turtles, Oscar and Parker, we rescued still reside here.

The wind creates small goosebumps on my arms. I can hear Mom's voice telling me she was always cold when she was younger too. The lake has transformed into a frozen blanket of water. The smell of gas fills the air as the snowmobiles rumble on the trails. I was always secretly afraid we would fall through the ice. I see Dad shoveling a snow path on the ice for our own personal rink, and mom tying our ice skates. I hear the sound of our laughter echoing across the silent lake as our inner tubes slide down the snowy hill.

A fish jumps, making ringlets on water, and I am brought back in the moment. Sitting in the kayak, I see The Great Blue Heron, and I know Mom is with me.

As the sun fades behind the tree line I am at peace. My grief comes and goes like the waves on Wazeecha. It is here I am reminded of all I have lost, but also all I have been given. It is here I can remember who I was before my Mother died. Just like time and seasons change these waters, my life has changed too. It is here I can accept that change.

It is on these waters, I know who I am again. I am a daughter of an amazing woman who was strong, courageous, and beautiful. It is here I know my Mother made a difference. She has left this Earth a much better place for having lived in it. I am inspired by her every day, and can remember here she wanted nothing more than for me to live my best life. It is here I learned by living again, I am honoring a beautiful life well lived.

On these waters I am at peace. On these waters cancer does not exist, but on these waters my Mother still does.

About the Author

Nicki Blucher Lives in Wisconsin with her husband, two children, and their dog named Aaron and bunny named Coco. After many years of working as a Customer Service Consultant, she is also now pursuing her lifelong passion for writing.

Nicki is a lifelong writer and first began creating characters and worlds in the second grade. She has always been able to connect personal emotions to pencil and paper. She has had poetry and personal essays published in the following collections: Bloodstone, Visions and Voices, Spirits in Motion, and the Best Poems and Poets.

She has an Associate in Applied Science degree in both Marketing and Human Resource Administration from Western Technical College, as well as a diploma in Writing from Long Ridge Writers Group.

When she isn't writing, you will find her enjoying the many adventures her children take her on. She enjoys swimming, camping, ice skating, sledding, watching football, and traveling. Nicki and her family are always planning their next exciting trip to experience.

During her career in the Customer Service field, Nicki has been able to connect with others and their stories. After the loss of her mother, she finally decided to get back to writing her first book. The book is about the grief of losing a parent and finding the strength and learning to embrace life after a loss that changes everything; which will outline Nicki's struggles of being a mother in a motherless world and her path of finding faith, strength, and courage to continue living.

To learn more about Nicki, please visit her at facebook.com/nickiblucherauthor/.

Journal

Journal

Journal

Journal

_____

_____

_____

_____

_____

_____

_____

_____

_____

Journal

References

Chapter 2

1.   (n.d.). Grief - MedicineNet. Retrieved March 31, 2020, from
https://www.medicinenet.com/loss_grief_and_bereavement/article.
htm

Chapter 6

1.   Schoeppel, K. (2013). *The Bible: The Truth About Psychics & Spiritual Gifts*. (1st Edition). United States of America.

Chapter 8

1.   (2017, July 5). 12 Science-Based Benefits of Meditation - Healthline. Retrieved April 5, 2020, from
https://www.healthline.com/nutrition/12-benefits-of-meditation

Chapter 10

1.   (2018, May 15). What Is Aromatherapy and How Does It Help Me? - Healthline. Retrieved April 3, 2020, from
https://www.healthline.com/health/what-is-aromatherapy
2.   (n.d.). 10 Healing Benefits of Aromatherapy – BoomBoom Naturals. Retrieved April 6, 2020, from
https://boomboomnaturals.com/blogs/news/10-healing-benefits-of-aromatherapy
3.   (n.d.). Essential Oils Guide: Safety | dōTERRA Essential Oils. Retrieved April 6, 2020, from
https://www.doterra.com/US/en/blog/healthy-living-essential-oils-guide-safety
4.   *The Essential Life*. (3rd Edition). (2017). United States of America.
5.   (2019, May 7). The Benefits of Burning Sage - Verywell

Mind. Retrieved April 1, 2020, from
https://www.verywellmind.com/the-benefits-of-burning-sage-4685244
6.   (n.d.). Palo Santo Benefits | Sacred Wood Essence. Retrieved April 6, 2020, from
https://sacredwoodessence.com/benefits/

Chapter 11

1.   Hall, J. (2003). *The Crystal Bible: A Definitive Guide to Crystals*. (1st Edition). Cincinnati, OH: Walking Stick Press.

Chapter 12

1.   (2014, July 18). Does energy healing really work? - NY Daily News. Retrieved March 7, 2020, from
https://www.nydailynews.com/life-style/health/energy-healing-work-article-1.1872210
2.   Judith, A. (2018). *Wheels of Life.* (2nd Edition). Woodbury, MN: Llewellyn Publications.
3.   (n.d.). Chakra One - Anodea Judith. Retrieved April 2, 2020, from https://anodeajudith.com/chakra-one/
4.   (n.d.). Chakra One - Anodea Judith. Retrieved April 2, 2020, from https://anodeajudith.com/chakra-two/
5.   (n.d.). Chakra One - Anodea Judith. Retrieved April 2, 2020, from https://anodeajudith.com/chakra-three/
6.   (n.d.). Chakra One - Anodea Judith. Retrieved April 2, 2020, from https://anodeajudith.com/chakra-four
7.   (n.d.). Chakra One - Anodea Judith. Retrieved April 2, 2020, from https://anodeajudith.com/chakra-five/
8.   (n.d.). Chakra One - Anodea Judith. Retrieved April 2, 2020, from https://anodeajudith.com/chakra-six/
9.   (n.d.). Chakra One - Anodea Judith. Retrieved April 2, 2020, from https://anodeajudith.com/chakra-seven/

Chapter 22

1.   (n.d.). Association for Death Education and .... Retrieved March 12, 2020, from http://adec.org/
2.   (n.d.). Center for Loss & Life Transition: Home. Retrieved March 12, 2020, from https://www.centerforloss.com/
3.   (n.d.). Grief.com - Help For Grief Because LOVE Never Dies. Retrieved March 14, 2020, from https://grief.com/
4.   (n.d.). Grief Resource Network. Retrieved March 14, 2020, from https://griefresourcenetwork.com/
5.   (n.d.). Hospice Foundation of America. Retrieved March 22, 2020, from https://hospicefoundation.org/
6.   (n.d.). Intuitive Spiritual Warrior Holistic Consulting & Healing™. Retrieved April 1, 2020, from https://www.intuitivespiritualwarrior.com/
7.   (n.d.). LJG Candles | Personalized Memorial Candles and Unique .... Retrieved March 22, 2020, from https://www.ljgcandles.com/
8.   (n.d.). Suicide Prevention Lifeline. Retrieved March 23, 2020, from https://suicidepreventionlifeline.org/
9.   (2019, November 6). National Helpline | SAMHSA - Substance Abuse and Mental .... Retrieved March 6, 2020, from https://www.samhsa.gov/find-help/national-helpline
10.   (n.d.). Open To Hope, Support for Dealing with Death, Grief, Loss .... Retrieved March 31, 2020, from https://www.opentohope.com/

About the Author

Kayla Brissi is a Certified Life Coach and Holistic Healing Practitioner, Marketing Strategist, Speaker, and International Bestselling Author.

She is the Owner and Founder of Kayla Brissi LLC and Intuitive Spiritual Warrior Holistic Consulting & Healing LLC.

Kayla is passionate about transforming lives around the world by sharing her unique message and gifts through multidimensional life coaching, holistic healing, marketing strategies and self-publishing consulting, inspirational speaking, and authorship.

She is the author of the bestselling book, *Healing from Grief*, and a co-author of several others that include #1 international bestseller, *Out of My Comfort Zone, The Beauty In My Mess (Vol I), Driven*, and *Dust to Salvation*. Kayla has also contributed to numerous industry publications and online platforms such as Thrive Global, Today.com, and Skillshare.

Kayla has an MBA with a finance concentration and a Bachelor of Arts degree with a double major in Accounting and Business Administration from Lakeland University, and a Financial Services Technical Diploma from Mid-State Technical College.

In her spare time, she is writing her next best-selling book, reading, watching movies, and spending time with her family.

To learn more about Kayla, please visit her website at
intuitivespiritualwarrior.com.

Join the Community

If you would like to receive a notification when my next book releases, receive free book promotions, behind the scenes access, information about upcoming events, sales, and receive exclusive discounts, join my online community by visiting my websites at intuitivespiritualwarrior.com or kaylabrissi.com.

Review Request

Please leave a review on Amazon! The number of reviews a book accumulates daily has a direct impact on how well it sells. Therefore, leaving a review, no matter its length, truly helps make it possible for me to continue releasing quality books and do what I do.

You can leave your review at https://www.amazon.com/dp/B086PQ7M25/.

Other Books by Kayla Brissi

The Beauty in My Mess: Stories of Truth, Transparencies and Triumphs (Vol I)

Over thirty courageous women joined together to tell a small piece of their autobiography that had a profound impact on their lives.

Within these pages, the authors have poured their hearts and souls into their stories by unveiling a time in their life where they had to find the deep inner strength, faith, and determination to see the beauty in their mess. They are stories of pain, healing, perseverance, and victory.

They are their stories for HIS glory!

Driven: A Guidebook By Women For Women; To Inspire and Empower

Women all across the world have come together to share their knowledge, joys, and pains of business, love, parenting, self-care, goal setting, finances and more.

This guidebook leaves no stone unturned to help you find your will to reach greater heights. You'll be ready to stop giving room to excuses and instead, you'll be ready to push forward in your dreams and truly crush your goals.

Out of My Comfort Zone: Stories of Courage, Perseverance and Victory

Out of My Comfort Zone features profiles from remarkable women of all backgrounds and places in life. Explore stories from business coaches, a publishing consultant, professional life-style bloggers, a marketing strategist, and educators from across the globe. Each of these rising entrepreneurs offers valuable insight on the struggles, challenges and life-changing moments that brought them success and personal satisfaction.

These remarkable women took risks, sought out challenges, and persevered in the face of adversity. By leaning into their passions and drive for success, they were able to change their lives.

Now, they share those stories – and advice – with others. Out of My Comfort Zone is a must read for all women, no matter their personal journey. Learn how ordinary women navigated hurdles and found the courage, perseverance, and determination to push through to beat the odds.

Dust to Salvation: Stories of Grace, Love, and Redemption in the Midst of Jesus Revealing Unexpected Miracles

Seven women are sharing their innermost secrets of failed relationships, health scares, infertility, and single parenting and they were brought together with one common bond. The undying love of Jesus Christ and how their lives are filled with hope for the future.

Independently, they discovered through prayer and unexpected friendships there was life beyond the brokenness that enveloped their hearts.